BEING BETTER AT BEING MARRIED

Building a Deeper Relationship Through Mutual Understanding

Ronald G. Joyner & Dr. Terry S. Smith

This book is dedicated to our wives
Sandra Joyner and Charlotte Smith
with whom we have each celebrated being married
for more than 50 years.

Contents

Foreword

Lots of marriages are in lots of trouble for lots of reasons. And there is no magic in a box that can fix what ails them.

My own experience says that many of the challenges to marriage lie in our unresolved personal issues. Why am I fearful? Why don't I take things seriously? What makes it so difficult for me to trust people? Why am I afraid to express my honest feelings? Why . . .

If people enter a relationship with the baggage of unidentified, unexplored, and unresolved issues of such magnitude, those things aren't going to be sorted out by virtue of a wedding ceremony. Then—horror of horrors—suppose that person marries someone who has his or her own bundle of issues that is equally large. Would you suspect there might be problems on the horizon? That the marriage could be threatened? That the relationship could fail? The hard-for-many-to-face truth is that *everybody* has baggage.

Ron Joyner, Terry Smith, and I have known each other for more than a quarter of a century. Terry and I were daily partners in Christian ministry for a dozen of those years. He was my primary resource to whom I would refer couples whose marriages were in trouble, and he was able to help an astonishing percentage of the people I sent his way.

The beginning point for Terry's work was getting to the Core Story of each of the partners—in order to help them better understand each other and their relationship. Understanding what was going on in the relationship was grounded in a clearer picture of self. If that insight seems simple and obvious to you, you are ahead of the majority of people who seem to think that "fixing my marriage" means "fixing my partner."

We all need fixing in one way or another. The surest way to maintain old, self-defeating patterns is to deny them. The best way to begin the process is with honest self-awareness.

What do I think and feel? Really? *Why* do I have these ideas and react as I do? Is there some *lie* I have absorbed about myself that sabotages how I deal with others? What *wound(s)* have been inflicted on me that are still festering? Are there *unhealthy coping mechanisms* I have evolved to avoid the pain of facing and dealing with those wounds?

After a few years of having person after person, couple after couple sent to him for help, Terry began training me to use some of the basic insights his training and experiences—very different as they were from mine—had given him. I have found his insights especially useful in premarital counseling of the many couples whose marriages I have officiated. Although I never got near Terry's ability to use the tools shared in this book that he and Ron have written, I learned enough to be helpful in a number of situations. You can learn to use them, too.

No, there is no magic box of tricks to fix marriages in jeopardy. But here are some insights and tools that can help. Thank you, Terry and Ron, for sharing them in an accessible format to help us toward the goal of being better at being married.

– Rubel Shelly, Ph.D.

Preface

To Those Who Want to Be Better at Being Married

Being married can be a richer, fuller experience when understanding, knowledge, and good approaches are used. The fact is many couples are not doing well. But there is a way to be better at being married! The purpose in writing this book is to help those who are discouraged restore enthusiasm in being together. We want to help reverse the tide for couples caught in the undertow of a deteriorating relationship.

Major relational disappointments have a devastating effect on being married. *How can this happen? What can be done? Who can help? Will things ever be right again?* These are important and legitimate questions, and my writing partner, Terry S. Smith, and I hope to provide some answers, starting with an overview of being married in Section 1.

You will be shown how to discover your personal story. You will see how life events have shaped the way you think and relate to others. In Section 2, you will find this process of personal story discovery explained in detail.

Discussions specific to communication are provided in Section 3. Communication is as vital to a relationship as blood is to the body. Focused and meaningful communication is necessary. Each person's voice matters as mutual understanding is cultivated between you and your spouse.

There are two working concepts for this book. The first is that a person's self-perception can unintentionally and without conscious awareness undermine being married. People can live with falsehoods they believe about themselves, but such false beliefs can interfere with establishing and maintaining strong relationships. Consider the following illustration of making "relational meringue."

Meringue is made from eggs. It's that thick, fluffy, white adornment on top of some desserts. Literally, this culinary wonder is nothing more than the white of an egg agitated so vigorously that tiny bubbles of air become trapped, creating a thick, fluffy dessert topping.

How meringue turns out for the cook is a direct function of the technique used to separate the egg. The key is to carefully break open the egg with as little trauma to the interior contents as possible and to meticulously separate the yolk from the white. Even the smallest amount of yolk in the egg white will act as a contaminant that will disrupt the physics and chemistry of creating meringue.

The yolk is a very concentrated substance. If there is even the slightest amount of yolk in the egg white, the meringue will not stand up.

There is no substitute for an egg in making genuine meringue, and in this is a great irony. Both what a cook needs to make good meringue and what will ruin good meringue are in the same egg, existing side by side.

Making meringue symbolically illustrates how being married can be contaminated by flawed personal beliefs. Influential and controlling beliefs can be flawed, and they can ruin an attempt to maintain a relationship. Your decisions and actions may not always be appropriate. Like making good meringue, you must be aware of and avoid the contaminants—the flawed beliefs—which can ruin a marital relationship.

The second working concept for this book, and the most difficult, is that both partners are individually responsible for working through any relational problems. One spouse cannot wait on or blame the other as an excuse for their inaction in addressing a problem.

This book is not intended to solve situations where character disorders, addictions, or any of the various neurotic and psychotic conditions underlie relational problems. These circumstances are rarely altered through self-help alone. Individual efforts in these cases need to be complemented by therapeutic support. This book is intended to provide facts and tools to bolster your own efforts at understanding yourself so that you can be better at being married.

We hope to help you identify any marital difficulties due in part to the existence of influential and controlling beliefs, ones that we call *Core Beliefs*. You will be introduced to a structured process of personal story-telling called the *Core Story*. This is a structured visual, emotional, and cognitive process designed to help you reconstruct and gain insight about the first eighteen years of your relational history, starting with when you were a child. Your Core Story experience will help you discover the origin of your Core Beliefs and their dominant influence on your relationships. Everything in this book, especially all of the conceptual backstory, is written to prepare you for identifying and understanding the significance of what you believe to be true.

In discovering your Core Beliefs, be on the lookout for *Core Lies*. Core Lies can result in so much misdirection in life. Core Lies are ill-formed Core Beliefs that often develop during early and middle childhood about such personal matters as safety, control, and self-esteem. What will be presented is how early-formed childhood misconceptions about maintaining relationships and appreciating personal value can carry over unmodified from childhood to adulthood.

Some Core Beliefs may form when we are an adult, but they rest upon the Core Beliefs developed during our early years of life. Core Beliefs are visceral, as they are tied to ideas—sometimes immature ideas—about such critical matters as physical, emotional, and social survival. This is precisely why the Core Story process and revisiting your childhood development can be so revelatory.

Powerful, controlling, immature, and dysfunctional Core Beliefs—Core Lies—can warp an adult's self-perception and thus mar a person's personality. Such misperceptions need to be identified and understood. Core Lies need to be replaced by *Core Truths*. This is a term we are using to identify correct and factual information. It is this reconnecting with your own story that will help you understand how your Core Beliefs came together and why they have such a profound influence on the way you see yourself and the way you relate to those around you.

You will be shown how first-formed Core Beliefs can arise out of early physical, emotional, or psychological trauma, which we will refer to as *Core Wounds*. Ill-formed Core Beliefs can also be the result of faulty information and bad examples. Children form Core Beliefs that help them get by, not to mature. Early-formed and ill-conceived Core Beliefs, if unaltered, can hold an adult emotionally hostage for life. A husband or wife can see themselves as entitled and invincible at one extreme or as threatened and worthless at the other. Mutual understanding, which is so important to being together, is hard to establish when motivating Core Beliefs remain hidden.

When trouble develops in being married, the typical reaction is to work harder and seek the culprit. Activity can replace substance, and exhaustion and blame are often the only measurable outcomes. In many cases of marital discord, the root of the problem is faulty thinking brought about by deficient Core Beliefs. There is no problem that cannot in some way be mitigated by the commitment of two people seeking out good information and working patiently and compassionately together.

As long as your self-perception (the views supported by your Core Beliefs) is not damaging to you and is in balance with the needs of your spouse and the demands of your circumstances, being married can be a meaningful and fulfilling experience. But when your self-perception becomes toxic for either you or your partner, the good life and the good aspects of being married will disintegrate. Distress will move into your home.

Your willingness to engage in self-examination, to commit to being accountable for your behavior, to develop a healthy view of yourself, and to courageously adapt in your relationship will provide you the keys to a rich married life.

I hope you will be motivated to seek the truth about yourself. Along with my writing partner, Terry S. Smith, I want to help you adapt to the needs of being married by building up your best self and, where necessary, educating your flawed self.

– Ronald G. Joyner

Preface

To Counselors, Ministers, and Life Coaches

Husbands and wives with problems being married are everywhere. We will attempt to provide you with some tools to help you determine if personal difficulties are tied to persistent childhood misperceptions. These Core Beliefs are influential and controlling beliefs that were established during early and middle childhood about such important matters as power and control, affection and esteem, and safety and security. These are a set of personally crafted, developmentally specific viewpoints that dictate how the people you are helping see themselves, their circumstances, and the relational obligations of being married. Core Beliefs will also determine how your people will interpret the information you present to them. This might be tricky as many of these Core Beliefs are beyond conscious awareness.

We will introduce in Section 2 a process of personal storytelling called the Core Story. This is a structured visual, emotional, and cognitive process of personal storytelling that is designed to help a person reconstruct and gain insight into the first eighteen years of their relational history. This process helps reveal the sources of Core Beliefs and illustrates their dominant influence in relationships.

We will also be presenting the components that impact the expression of personality, especially as this expression affects being married. The model we present is not intended to replace or compete with any other models of personality that may exist. We only want to reinforce how Core Beliefs affect the ultimate expression of personality while being married.

Everything in this book, especially the conceptual back story, is written to prepare people to identify and understand the significance of their Core Beliefs, as well as the influence of these Core Beliefs on being married.

Some of you mentor and life coach while others offer a more therapeutic or pastoral approach to help those coming to you. Our intent is not to address problems caused by character disorders, addictions, or neurotic and psychotic conditions. This book is intended to provide you with perspectives and tools to help you better reach those coming to you who only need to gain a better self-understanding to be better at being married.

We hope you will gain insights that will equip you to better present objective feedback, helpful information, and goal setting to your clients. These insights can be helpful in augmenting therapeutic approaches that range from traditional Freudian-based psychoanalysis to techniques influenced by more contemporary behavioral, cognitive, and acceptance and commitment theories of psychotherapy.

You may also find the material contained in Section 3 to be helpful for use in aftercare, seminars, classes, or facilitated small group discussions. This section has fifty-two topic-specific discussions that can serve as the basis for structured weekly communication between spouses on topics relevant to being married. Sources for reliable information along with a list of recommended books are provided at the end of this book.

There is one thing that every married individual has in common: their self-perception as influenced by unconscious Core Beliefs is very determinate in how they will behave in life. Consider the following testimonial.

A STORY FROM TERRY: MY BLIND SPOT

After only being married a few years, I received a call from my wife while at work. She said to me, "I am leaving you." I responded, "I will be right home!" Once at home I asked her what was happening. She said she would not let our 2-year-old and 10-month-old daughters stay with my mother, as I had planned for them while my wife and I attended a college retreat together. I had just recently reconnected with my mother, an alcoholic from whom I had been estranged for eighteen years and who had been sober for only two weeks.

Well, I had not previously listened to my wife's concerns about my mother. I had not considered the possible danger of my children staying with her. I just wanted my mother to feel like a part of my family. I had not differentiated my role as a parent from my over-responsible self-perception as one who is obligated to save other people.

My self-perception supported the misperception that I was responsible for fixing other people's problems. I accepted my wife's concerns, and she and I worked together to make alternative arrangements for the care of our children.

· · · · ·

Ideally, powerful and controlling Core Beliefs mature as a person grows older, learns more, experiences more, and becomes wiser. This doesn't always happen. Trauma (which we are calling a Core Wound), environment, socialization, and education may stunt Core Belief maturation. Misinformation and untruths will have significant influence over your client's self-perception—on how they handle stress, work through problems, and relate to others. These we are calling Core Lies.

How you interpret what your client tells you might also be affected by your own early-formed Core Beliefs. Core Beliefs rule us all because these unconscious "rules of the road" will determine how we see ourselves, how we process what we hear, how we interpret what we see, how we solve problems, and how we treat other people. It will be best to understand your own Core Beliefs and Core Story first so it will not affect the process of assisting others.

Unless your client's controlling Core Beliefs are explored and taken into account, your best efforts and those of your client to restore failing relationships, correct bad decision-making, reduce destructive behavior, adjust a warped self-perception, and improve being married will be hindered.

Core Beliefs will not be altered by information just because the information is correct. Stimulating a personal assessment of Core Beliefs requires stimulating the conscious awareness of a client or client couple. Until a person trusts in and accepts the relevance of potentially transformative information that is beyond their own knowledge and experience, a change in their Core Beliefs, especially a Core Lie, will not occur. Where there is not trust, there will be resistance to embracing new information and changing ways of thinking even if the effects of a Core Lie are being disruptive.

One final tool for your consideration is the recognition and use of your clients' spiritual space. The spiritual element is one of the five dimensions of personality that also includes the mental, physical, social, and emotional aspects of life. Each of these elements plays a part in defining a person's psychological landscape. To ignore any one of these during a program of coaching or counseling is much like a blind man trying to decide what a whole elephant looks like after only feeling the big, floppy ears or the rough, thick skin.

Too often the spiritual is contaminated by a client's or the practitioner's experience with religious dogma and church members. The spiritual aspects of life are then discounted as being too abstract, too contrived, or too intrusive. Admittedly, some people's experience with religion has been disastrous, but that should not devalue the need to explore the spiritual element of personality during interaction with a client.

The challenge for you, whether acting as a coach or therapist, is how to best offer holistic support to your clients. Helping your client muster the courage and confidence to accept and put into action the wisdom offered by others will result in a better quality of life for your clients, a revival of being married, and an overall improvement in the outcomes experienced by the people you are trying to help.

– Dr. Terry S. Smith

Acknowledgements

The authors want to thank Charlotte Durham and Rebekah Jenkins Gibbs for their editorial contributions, F. Joseph McLaughlin, Ph.D., Associate Professor of the Practice of Psychology and Human Development at Vanderbilt University, for his helpful critique, and Chad Harrington for his services as Publishing Project Manager.

Our wives, Sandra Joyner and Charlotte Smith, also deserve recognition for their encouragement and support of our efforts and for the many suggestions made to improve what we were attempting to clearly communicate.

Most of all we want to gratefully acknowledge the thousands of people over the past thirty-five years who have graciously allowed Terry Smith to listen to their individual Core Story and to witness their individual greatness and overcoming spirit.

Introduction

The compatibilities necessary for those who are married are in many ways the same as those required for two people trying to co-author a book. To work effectively together there must be mutual respect and a shared vision for what is to be accomplished. Both parties in the relationship must be willing to communicate, coordinate, and compromise.

Opposites can work well together if they recognize the value of their differences. Terry is athletic while Ron is not. Ron was an intellectual nerd growing up, and Terry was not. Ron thinks in words while Terry thinks in pictures.

When Terry reads a book, he puts it down if not captured by a story in the first chapter. Ron reads a book cover-to-cover in order to discover the entirety of the author's purpose. Ron likes to read books that are instructive and lead him to reasonable, useful conclusions. Terry prefers books that speak to him where he lives. Terry intuits well. Ron reasons well.

We are in many ways an odd collaborative match, but what we do share in common is our pursuit of what is true. Ron's intellectual quest for truth has led him to relational integrity. Terry's relational quest for truth and academic excellence has led him to intellectual integrity.

Through our joint effort we hope to give you a good three-dimensional view of how to better understand yourself in the context of being married. We both want you to finish this book with a much better understanding of your personal story, what is being referred to as your Core Story, and how your story impacts how you feel about yourself and about being married.

People communicate and learn differently, so we have worked together to make this book appealing to both left-brained and right-brained readers. To this end, this book provides an experiential taste of what we are trying to say through sharing stories, while also presenting the details about the significance of the Core Story, Core Beliefs, Core Wounds, Core Lies, and the Core Truths and their relevance to being married. For those who may prefer to start with reading the stories and illustrations, these can be found on pages 22, 31, 33, 38, 42, 43, 45, 53, 59, 64, 90, 92, 96, and 98 and are designated by this icon:

Many couples look on marriage as a third party in their relationship. They talk about marriage as if it has a life of its own. Problems in their relationship are blamed on the marriage as if it were a disagreeable neighbor. Marriage as a term has taken on a decidedly institutional connotation. Marriage counseling will be sought to find out what is wrong with the marriage, not what is wrong with those who are married.

This book addresses personal beliefs and how they affect the relational bonds inherent to being married. We will explore how a beneficial and fulfilling marital relationship is rooted in mutual respect and understanding. We hope to guide you toward the realization that what emerges from being married is a whole that is greater than the sum of its parts. Being married involves the impact that the personalities of two people have upon one another. This special relationship requires establishing a quality of communication, developing a level of trust, and maintaining a degree of mutual understanding that results in functional unity. If there is a problem between a husband and a wife, the problem is with one or both of them, not with the marriage.

Being married is a complicated subject to write about. Asking you to examine your influence on being married is a difficult request. Deeply held personal feelings create an emotional barrier that is hard to break through even with helpful information. Even if desperate for something to change, married couples are nonetheless guarded about who and what can be trusted to provide guidance for them. We hope to provide information in this book that can be both useful and trusted.

Many books and articles written about being married focus on defining the desirable attributes of this very special relationship. Workshops encourage participants to adopt behaviors that might help reduce conflict, enhance feelings of intimacy, and improve communication. This book is different. We will put forth that how you think will determine how you behave, regardless of how much you know about how you would like to act. Our experience has been this: until you get in touch with your personal story, until you get in touch with how and why you think as you do, and until you identify the beliefs that control you, attempts to improve the part you play in being married are not likely to be as successful as you would like.

Pay attention! We are trying to influence you and open your mind to new ways of thinking. You need to be cautious about any effort by anyone to challenge what you think and how you think. We invite your close scrutiny of everything we have written.

Our intention is to raise your awareness about how your behavior is affected more by what you believe than by what you know. We want to provide you with good information and some tools to assist you with self-inquiry. We want to help you identify if you believe influential misinformation, or what we are calling a Core Lie, then encourage you to replace it with a Core Truth, which is the term we are using for factual, trustworthy information. In no way is our intention to tell you what your beliefs should be. We are not trying to recruit you or sell anything. You are not being asked to join anything, and we are not seeking financial donations. We are only promoting a thoughtful examination by you of your Core Beliefs, or your most influential and controlling beliefs, and your consideration of how these Core Beliefs are impacting your being married.

Our intention is to raise your awareness about how your behavior is affected more by what you believe than by what you know.

It is difficult, if not impossible, for you to alter your life view by simply trying to emulate something read in a book or heard in a workshop. As a child, you interpreted the world around you as best you could and decided with a child's mind how to navigate within your situation as you experienced it. These early-formed beliefs established how you interpreted matters related to power and control, safety and security, and attracting and holding onto affection and esteem. Many of these initial beliefs formed in early and middle childhood can still exist within you, relatively unchanged, as an adult.

Some of what you chose to believe about yourself and the world around you was good and helpful; some of what you came to believe was incorrect. Children are keen observers but not always the best interpreters! To make matters even more complicated, most early-formed, controlling Core Beliefs end up beyond the conscious awareness of the adult and cannot be accessed without a special effort such as that detailed in Section 2. As you will see in more detail in Chapters 3 and 4, the operation of Core Beliefs can work in one of three ways—help you maintain emotional and relational balance, result in misdirected motivations, or cause you to have a very low opinion of yourself.

Until you come to understand your life view as determined by what you believe, hearing or reading about how you should behave will largely be a waste of time. Sustained changes in behavior, as evidenced through the personality, are brought about by a change of heart, not by more information. What you believe will always overrule what you know!

This story from Terry shares how strongly-held, truth-based, shared beliefs can be very stabilizing to the relationship of a married couple.

A STORY FROM TERRY: WHO IS RESPONSIBLE?

While driving home one evening, listening to a call-in radio talk show, the host of the program posed this question, "Why are so many couples getting a divorce?" After many people responded with answers such as "the chemistry is gone" or "we seem to be going in different directions" or "she no longer makes me happy" or "things have just changed" or "it no longer works," the talk show host said in exasperation, "I am tired of hearing this! Is anyone out there having a good time being married?"

I decided to call. After getting him on the line, telling him my name and that I was the father of four children, a grandparent, and that I had been married for over thirty years, the talk show host asked me this question: "Do you have anything to say?"

I said, "I think I do! I don't make my wife responsible for my happiness! I own that!"

It got really quiet. I shared with him that she was my best friend and soul mate. I told him we have faced together those relational issues common to being married. I told him we sought to understand each other before trying to be understood during difficult times. I said our goal was always to build on a foundation of mutual respect and personal accountability. I told him we were determined not to permit a co-dependent relationship to develop where one was expected to meet the unmet needs and one-sided expectations of the other. Finally, I said this approach to being married has worked well for my wife and me.

• • • • •

Even intense counseling sessions led by capable professionals cannot bring about the necessary changes in a relationship until any immature, dysfunctional, controlling Core Beliefs—the Core Lies—are identified and modified to become supportive of new relationship-building attitudes and behaviors. Deeply held childhood impressions housed beyond conscious awareness will not surrender easily. This is why a structured self-inquiry such as that which is provided through the Core Story process can be a crucial step toward a better understanding of the origins of the way you think and what you believe to be true.

Our contention is that if you are "stuck," meaning you can't move on and you can't dig out of a marital problem, then you should search for any Core Lies that may be contributing to your relational or self-esteem problems. This exploration is done in order for you to determine when and why your behavior at times might be self-serving, self-deprecating, or dismissive of the needs of your spouse. You might think you are deserving and entitled, but on the other hand you could see yourself as unworthy or not good enough. You might feel invincible or you could feel particularly vulnerable or expendable. You might see yourself as adorable and very attractive or you could see yourself as undesirable and flawed. If you are "stuck," you need to find the problem. The Core Story process as detailed in Section 2 can help.

Faulty, controlling beliefs will not permit you to make any meaningful changes in your behavior until your Core Lies are exposed, understood, and replaced with Core Truths.

We have not written this book to be a pep talk but a reality check about being married. Your Core Beliefs about who you are and how the world works will prevail in every important decision you make. If these controlling beliefs are faulty due to bad experience or bad information, and if they are in reality Core Lies, then your attempts to emulate good examples for being married as outlined in books, identified in workshops, or suggested by counselors will be self-sabotaged. Faulty, controlling beliefs will not permit you to make any meaningful changes in your behavior until your Core Lies are exposed, understood, and replaced with Core Truths. This is why the Core Story process is so important.

Discovering and understanding controlling Core Beliefs, beliefs which determine your self-perception and are expressed through your personality, is work that only you can do. The need for you to do work within the mental, emotional, and spiritual dimensions of your personality is the challenge that makes this book very different. A great deal of this book is devoted to the childhood development of Core Beliefs because a better understanding of the child helps to better understand the adult.

We have found that many people are disabled in their ability to think and act appropriately because inaccurate Core Beliefs dominate their self-perception. They see themselves and their circumstances in such a way that makes it difficult for them to interpret the real-time relational and structural needs of being married.

This book will challenge you—unlike many others—as it is designed to provide good information, direction, encouragement, and the tools necessary to aid you on a journey of self-discovery and personal transformation. Our goal is for you to embrace the challenge of change, to seek out trusted sources of new information, and to accept that information alone will not replace deep-seated beliefs.

The approach we have taken in this book is to be concise and practical. The goal of this book is to take you to the next level in being married and see it as being much more than mutual compatibility. Mending trouble or reducing strains in being married will involve going deep into the foundational elements of your personality.

Beginning in Section 1, Chapter 1 will present a concept of the structure of personality and will highlight how Core Beliefs are influential in determining how people function relationally in being married. In Chapter 2, we will establish how individually held Core Beliefs dominate your self-perception. We will show that actions based on these beliefs can either build up or tear down a relationship. Chapter 3 will explore how and why Core Beliefs are formed in childhood and often persist into adulthood. Chapter 4 will explain in more depth the power of Core Beliefs and the dominance of Core Lies.

Chapters 5 and 6 will complement Section 2 by introducing the life story of one of the authors, Terry S. Smith, and relating the information revealed in this story to the Core Story process. We will emphasize the Core Story process as a means by which you can discover and better understand the contribution that your childhood and your family of origin has had on the formulation of your Core Beliefs about safety, security, self-esteem, power, and control. Your Core Story will provide a path for a better understanding of your self-perception, as expressed through your personality, by aiding in the exposure of any Core Lies so that they can be corrected. We hope to help you create a path for your Core Lies to be replaced by Core Truths.

Chapter 7 will show ways that unity in being married is influenced by self-perception and how unity can be achieved without the loss of individuality. The importance of substantive communication will be stressed. Finally, Chapter 8 will outline a pathway for meaningful change and will stress the importance of engaging the spiritual dimension of your personality. In this chapter, we will explore the many elements involved in the process of personal transformation, and then we will move on to Sections 2 and 3, where tools will be provided to help you as you move toward self-discovery and a higher level of understanding between you and your spouse.

This book can help you as long as you invest the time to do the work that is needed. Personal transformation is not a passive exercise. Personal transformation is more than just knowing or desiring; it is the act of becoming. Personal transformation is a process that takes place in the spiritual domain of your personality. You have to juxtapose the significance of self-sovereignty against the significance of what you should follow and who you should serve.

> *Personal transformation requires thorough and honest self-reflection and the courage to challenge and educate misinformed Core Beliefs by embracing Core Truths.*

Personal transformation requires thorough and honest self-reflection and the courage to challenge and educate misinformed Core Beliefs by embracing Core Truths. It is within your spiritual domain that you will weigh the price you are willing to pay for what you want and what you expect to get in return for what you give. It is within the spiritual domain of your life that you will decide how much of your interaction with others will be self-serving and pragmatic and how much will be nurturing and generous.

For this book to make any difference in your life, you must be courageous enough to be open, honest, and objective about yourself, teachable enough to accept new information and new ideas, and humble enough to be open to personal change as an option for improvement in being married.

The Influence of Core Beliefs on Being Married

"By wisdom a house is built, and through understanding it is established." – Proverbs 24:30

CHAPTER 1

Personality Development

Attraction to someone and the ability to establish and maintain a meaningful, fulfilling, and enduring relationship boils down to the compatibility of two personalities. With this in mind, a workable understanding of both the structure and dynamics of personality will help you to establish a context for learning how Core Beliefs impact personality and being married. As personality is developing during early and middle childhood, influential information and experiences are processed psychologically. These influences impact the formation of physical, mental, social, emotional, and spiritual concepts. It is with the contributions made by these five dimensions of personality that Core Beliefs are formed, and it is these Core Beliefs that underlie the development of a person's self-perception as evidenced through their personality.

Consider this visual as an aid to help you while you are reading this chapter.

PERSONALITY			
SELF-PERCEPTION			
CORE BELIEFS			
Spiritual Dimension			
Physical Dimension	Mental Dimension	Social Dimension	Emotional Dimension
INFLUENCE			

You will notice in our concept model for personality that there is a very open and free-flowing connection between the physical, mental, social, emotional, and spiritual dimensions of personality and the layer of Core Beliefs. This depiction of proximity and connectedness is deliberate. We are calling this gray area in the model the Zone of Deliberation.

When consideration is being given to a new influence or to reprocessing what is already held as a Core Belief, there is considerable interaction at both a conscious and an unconscious level within this Zone of Deliberation. For example, awareness of your physical state is a function of the mental dimension, but establishing the meaning of this awareness involves the spiritual dimension. Likewise, you think about a lot of things, but the significance of what you are thinking about is a spiritual determination. You have lots of friends, but the value of these friendships is a spiritual input. There are emotions that are attendant to each of the physical, mental, and social dimensions of personality, but the appropriateness of these feelings is determined by the spiritual dimension of personality. All of these interactions will be additionally affected by previous psychic determinations that are preserved within the Core Beliefs.

You think about a lot of things, but the significance of what you are thinking about is a spiritual determination.

Our concept of personality and the model we are using are not exhaustive nor are they intended to replace any of the many other concepts and models used to explain personality. Our model is intended strictly to serve as a conceptual tool to aid you in following the points we are trying to make. In the following chapters we will develop in much more detail how we believe self-perception, Core Beliefs, personal story discovery, marital unity, and insight-directed transformation fit into our concept of personality.

Tendencies of personality are certainly influenced by many genetic determinates. How many times have you heard, "You are just like your mom or just like your dad?" But influence is the raw material for the formation of a person's personality, notwithstanding genetic predispositions. Influence for our purposes consists of the information, observations, and experiences that we are all exposed to as human beings. The source of these influences can come from family, friends, school, place of worship, and various forms of media, as well as from interactions with the local community and the broader culture. The influences that come into a person's life are sometimes invited, but just as often, especially for children, they are random, arbitrary, and possibly ill-timed.

THREE ILLUSTRATIONS: THE IMPACT OF EARLY NEGATIVE INFLUENCES

A wife we will call Marjorie does not feel attractive and as a result does not know how to adequately respond to her husband's expressions of affection. When she was young, other children made fun of her being overweight. Because of this early ridicule, even though Marjorie lost weight in her late teens she had already developed a controlling Core Belief, a Core Lie, that she was ugly. As a young child her spiritual development was not robust enough for her to override these negative influences and formulate instead a well-formed idea of her self-worth and personal significance. She was unable to detoxify the negative influence brought about by the early ridicule of her peers, so she internalized this ridicule as a Core Lie that she is unattractive.

Susan is dyslexic. She struggled in school with bad grades because she did not test well. In comparison to her peers, Susan felt stupid. She converted this feeling into a Core Lie that she could not succeed. By adulthood, Susan had learned how to compensate for her reading disability and went on to complete a college degree and retain a good job. But her misinformed Core Belief, her Core Lie, persisted, and she continued to lack self-confidence when making decisions. Susan was intelligent and very relatable, but she could not see her own good qualities. Like Marjorie in the illustration above, she too had not developed enough spiritually as a child to counteract the formulation of her Core Lie with a Core Truth that she is actually very capable.

A husband we will call Pete is often prone to lie in order to cover his mistakes or to exaggerate even the least of his accomplishments. This element of Pete's personality makes his wife not necessarily trust what he tells her. This behavior is a source of conflict. This behavior is the result of early parental conditioning and the formation of a Core Belief, really a Core Lie, that failure in life is not an option. Pete had developed a Core Belief that success is the ultimate measure of self-worth, and that truth is something not to be honored but manufactured as a mechanism of self-defense.

* * * * *

These illustrations make an important point that is emphasized throughout this book: Core Beliefs, if not developmentally mature and free of misinformation, misinterpretation, and traumatic fixation, can contribute to personality problems and create relational stress that can adversely affect being married. This is why we are placing such emphasis on the very important role of the spiritual dimension in the expression of an adult's personality. Spiritual development embodies the formation of ideas about significance, compassion, authority, prudence, duty, forgiveness, fidelity, respect, and obedience. The spiritual dimension is where we house our concepts of fellowship and our sense of the esthetic. Spiritual concepts are what temper the sometimes primal inclination of the other dimensions of personality toward self-will. It is the important role in healing Core Wounds and replacing Core Lies with Core Truths that the depth, breadth, quality, and timing of the education of the spiritual dimension is so critical.

Core Beliefs, if not developmentally mature and free of misinformation, misinterpretation, and traumatic fixation, can contribute to personality problems and create relational stress that can adversely affect being married.

Life is a process of undoing and reassembly, of destruction and repair. For too many this process is one-sided—too much undoing, too much destruction, too much of what does not work, and a lack of recovery. Some people are so immersed in their circumstances, so reinforced in faulty ways of thinking and acting, and so underdeveloped spiritually that they cannot see their way to a better life or to being better at being married. For so many there seems to be no path out of their suffering and unhappiness.

Sometimes it will take more than physical stamina, mental dexterity, affability, and steady nerves for you to tackle life's challenges. Sometimes it will take something extra but within your reach to be able to muster the resolve to make changes in some of the ways you think and act. Sometimes it will take you turning to the spiritual dimension of your personality to find the strength and direction needed to move forward.

It is within the spiritual dimension of personality that we do some of our best emotional work. For instance, to the extent married couples are able to subdue and constructively channel tendencies toward self-will they are able to work together cooperatively for the sake of making decisions that are in the best interest of the entire family. Consider the illustration that follows.

AN ILLUSTRATION: SPIRITUALLY MEDIATED DECISIONS

Couples making joint decisions may have differing beliefs and preferences, but a spiritual ethic of cooperation is what will make possible self-will being set aside for the sake of coordination and compromise. Consider all the factors of personality that each parent will bring to the table in making a decision about where their children might attend school. Each parent's own experience with being in school, along with what is known about the school system, geography, local demographics, and the aptitude or special needs of a child will all be factors in making such a decision. Each parent's Core Beliefs about such things as freedom of choice and social standing will come into play. Preferences about curriculum and religion, the overall value placed upon education, the family traditions of each parent, social pressure, and economic status are but a few of the many factors that will need to be processed and agreed upon by a couple in developing a plan for the education of their children. Being aware and respectful of each one's personality traits, specifically their Core Beliefs, will go a long way in permitting couples to work together more harmoniously in making decisions.

●　●　●　●　●

One reason that Core Beliefs can sabotage a needed collaboration like the one just illustrated is that these important, controlling ideas begin to form early in life and can remain unchanged into adulthood. Young children are very limited in the degree to which this very important spiritual dimension of their personality has developed, so as a result they are limited in their ability to evaluate the significance of how they are being influenced. The Core Beliefs of the young are usually formed as a result of chance and circumstance with little supervision by their immature and under-educated spiritual dimension. The influences in early and middle childhood impact the physical, mental, social, and emotional domains of impressionable personalities and pass mostly unedited and unfiltered through an underdeveloped spiritual dimension to influence the initial formation of critical Core Beliefs. If these early influences are positive, then the impressions created will more likely result in the formation of Core Beliefs that will support the development of a healthy self-perception. If the early influences are bad, such unfortunate, early persuasions can have a damaging effect on the formation of early Core Beliefs and provide an environment for the persistence of Core Lies later in life.

Identifying and modifying any dysfunctional, misinformed, or trauma-induced Core Beliefs are commitments that are best accomplished by doing spiritual work. As the personality diagram appearing earlier in this chapter depicts, the spiritual dimension spans all the other elements within the Zone of Deliberation of the personality. But change is hard work, so there needs to be a source of energy that will motivate the learning, challenging, and adapting that must take place if any meaningful changes in thinking and personal behavior is to take place. Faith is this source of energy.

Faith is the commitment to an idea that is necessary to break through the doubt and misinformation that discourages new thinking. It is new thinking that creates more choices for us, and with more choices we can all better resolve issues relating to fear, insecurity, guilt, shame, failure, worth, integrity, etc. It is the feeling that we have few choices or no choices that so often is the basis for despair. Faith is the phenomenon that takes place within the spiritual domain that neutralizes the risks perceived in substituting one belief for another.

Faith is the phenomenon that takes place within the spiritual domain that neutralizes the risks perceived in substituting one belief for another.

Faith is often associated with religion, but faith is not exclusive to religion. Faith results when you place a high level of spiritual significance to a piece of information. Through faith you become willing to bypass doubt or concern and assume the psychic risk of aligning yourself with a new way of thinking. It will take spiritual work to displace any dysfunctional or misinformed Core Beliefs that may be affecting your enjoyment of life and success in being married.

The development of personality as a child becomes the maintenance of personality as an adult. Throughout life, the spiritual dimension will remain an important mediator between the impact that various influences have on an individual's self-perception, and thus their personality. The spiritual dimension will create the pathway for new insight to bring about changes in existing Core Beliefs. The spiritual dimension of personality is what creates an appetite for Core Truths.

Core Truths are information that is real and relevant. It can be found in the honest and thorough pursuit of information that is tested and trustworthy. Core Truths are the antidote for Core Beliefs fraught with prejudice, illusion, misinformation, misinterpretation or that have been trauma induced. Core Truths are easily available but not always easily accepted.

We have a single goal for you. We want you to be able to read your circumstances, assess your situation, learn your personal story, become aware of what controls and motivates your behavior (especially in being married), and be able to effectively identify and embrace Core Truths for your life.

CHAPTER 2

The Dominance of Self-Perception

Most individuals who become married are filled with hope and excitement over the prospect of sharing their life with someone very special. In the absence of coercion from any social, family, religious, or economic pressure, people are typically drawn together to marry by a deep and special attraction to one another.

Factors related to physical appearance, shared interests, intelligence, personality, family, career, or religion initially attract two people to one another with the mutual expectation that life will be better for them as a couple. Unfortunately, what was appealing about a person in the beginning may not be enough to provide what the relationship will need over the long-run.

The nature and depth of communication will change; expectations will be challenged; roles will be redefined. New relational skills will need to be learned, accommodations and compromises will have to be made, sacrifices will be required, apologies and forgiveness will be necessary, and losses will be suffered. The reality of trying to live in harmony as a couple is more difficult than having fun on a date.

The dynamics of being married are very intricate. There are many moving parts to this unique relationship. The personal demands can be taxing at times, and these challenges will either reveal your best side or flush out your worst side. Being married will not stay where it began. Both partners will need to evolve developmentally over time because coping that worked one way at one time will not work at another time as individual preferences and capabilities change.

It is inevitable that the magic that accompanies the newness, novelty, and naiveté of the early years will give way to the reality of both a husband and wife emerging to be as they really are. Being married will expose a couple's weaknesses. Sometimes this shake out in personality will be accommodated and no big deal; at other times, it will be a big reveal!

> *It is inevitable that the magic that accompanies the newness, novelty, and naiveté of the early years will give way to the reality of both a husband and wife emerging to be as they really are.*

This story by Terry details a specific time when views of significance and equality became a source of relational conflict.

A STORY FROM TERRY: WHAT YOU SEE IS DETERMINED BY WHERE YOU SIT

After thirty years of being married, communication between me and my wife was breaking down. We wanted things to get better, so we went to counseling. During our first session, my wife, Charlotte, was asked to draw a picture of how she experienced our relationship. The picture was one of her standing at the kitchen sink wearing an apron while washing dishes. She drew me in a graduate's cap and gown with a doctoral diploma in my hand with a caption over my head that read, "What does she know?"

I was shocked! She said that when she shared a thought, a feeling, or made a suggestion, my response was often, "Well, did you ever consider . . . ." She felt she was being discounted because she was less educated by having only an undergraduate degree—with honors I might add. I perceived that I had a lot to offer her because of my extensive studies in human personality. All she really wanted was for me to validate her point of view by listening and considering she could be right. I shared my intent, she shared her feeling of being discounted, and we both made adjustments in the way we perceived ourselves and in the way we communicated with one another. Self-perception works both ways—how you see yourself and how you see your mate. A faulty impression either way can bring conflict into the relationship.

● ● ● ● ●

Taking into account the complexity of being married, we have tried to isolate one factor that might contribute more than any other to the relationship being either very fulfilling or drifting toward disaster. Our experience has led us both to believe that self-perception is the factor to emphasize.

Let us be very clear about what is meant by the term self-perception. Self-perception is our own prophesy about ourselves. We become who we think we are, and this can be a good thing or something very limiting. Self-perception is how we view both our inside world and the world outside. It is what we use to gauge any situation and decide how we will respond. It is our concept of who we think we are and how we think others see us.

Self-perception is how we view both our inside world and the world outside.

Self-perception actually exists in two different but interrelated levels of our psyche. First, there is living our lives based upon an awareness of what we are thinking. This is our conscious state of mind where our thoughts and actions are purposeful, directed, deliberate, thoughtful, calculated, and intentional.

Then there is the unconscious state of mind. Here we have no conscious awareness of what we are thinking, and this is the level where Core Beliefs have the most significant—and sometimes the most troublesome—impact. Core Beliefs centered on power, significance, and safety have tremendous influence on self-perception. The problem is—and this is a major point of emphasis for this book—that the origin, context, and content of these powerfully influential Core Beliefs may not be consciously recognizable to us.

Core Beliefs, and thus self-perception, are greatly influenced in their formation and expression by a universal desire for self-preservation. There is and will always be a dynamic tension between protecting our perceived self-interest and opening ourselves up to a more inclusive worldview where the well-being of others equals or exceeds our own.

Self-preservation is one of the first things that concerns us as human beings. Through the process of maturation, ideas about self-preservation should become more sophisticated, more contextual in nature, and ideally we become more considerate of others. Maturation should frame our self-interest so that it is placed into context with our obligations as an adult member of social, civic, spiritual, professional, and family communities.

What if this maturation does not happen? What if you didn't advance in your thinking as you grew older? What if emotional trauma has burned early-formed Core Beliefs into your mind as the only way you can allow yourself to think? What if information you were given as a child, or information that you interpreted to be true, was bad from the beginning? What if a lack of education, opportunity, or experience did not correct bad information as you grew older?

The answers to all these questions will determine the quality and character of how you see yourself, how well you relate to others, and how successful you will be at being married.

Our self-perception involves what we believe is necessary to stay in control, to be safe, and to be liked. Self-perception can permit us to see things as they really are, or it can result in a distortion of what is actually going on and how to respond properly. Flawed self-perception can cause such extremes in behavior as total self-centeredness on one hand and self-loathing on the other.

As you mature in being married, the vision of self should begin to evolve so that it begins to function more as a vision of mutual self-interest. This is not to say you should surrender your identity and individuality, or that you cannot have your own interests and preferences. Being married at its best is when your perceived needs and those of your spouse are being fulfilled in harmony rather than in competition with one another. This state can also be referred to as unity or oneness. The topic of unity will be covered more thoroughly in Chapter 7.

Self-centeredness and a partnership with another person mix like oil and water. A distortion in self-perception, what will be referred to as a Core Lie, will be unrelenting in undermining the attempts of a couple to cultivate a spirit of trust, unity, and shared purpose. We hope to provide you in Section 2 with a tool to help you identify the controlling Core Beliefs that color your self-perception and to help you mark any Core Lies which need to be replaced with Core Truths.

A distortion in self-perception, what will be referred to as a Core Lie, will be unrelenting in undermining the attempts of a couple to cultivate a spirit of trust, unity, and shared purpose.

The search for Core Beliefs must use a very deliberate, objective, directed, and proven process because these beliefs exist without conscious awareness. These controlling beliefs must be brought into the light of consciousness because they ultimately rule how you see who you are, how you know what you need, and how you relate to others and their needs. Our goal is to help you keep a Core Lie from sabotaging your efforts to be a good marital partner.

Self-perception, a major contributor to our expectations, drives a couple to marry in the first place. In order to marry, both a husband and wife must first believe they are a qualified recipient and a capable giver of love. They must also share a common expectation that within an ongoing relationship they will realize such benefits as acquiring a compatible companion, achieving parenthood, obtaining an earnings partner, and enjoying a monogamous and consensual sexual relationship. But what happens when there is an extended separation, illness, infertility, career resentment, bankruptcy, or sexual dysfunction? The list could go on and on. Disillusionment sets in when the realities of life begin to challenge the expectation of what being married should be like.

A dominating Core Lie that renders you inflexible produces a relational blind spot. Seeing your point of view as the best view in every situation is to ignore the possibility that information you need is yet to be learned or can best be provided by someone else. Just as the inability to bend will cause a stick to break, inflexibility can also cause marital bonds to break.

Consider this illustration of the influence Core Beliefs have over one's self-perception and the damage that a flawed self-perception, a Core Lie, can cause.

AN ILLUSTRATION: FLYING WITH INSTRUMENTS

The pilot of a private aircraft is licensed at the basic level to fly VFR, meaning to fly by Visual Flight Rules. This is a circumstance where a pilot will be able to keep the aircraft properly oriented only if the horizon is visible. Pilots flying at this level of training are dependent upon using what they can see of the horizon for orientation.

In order to fly in inclement weather where the horizon is not visible, a pilot must be specially trained and additionally certified to fly IFR, meaning to fly by Instrument Flight Rules. In this instance, a pilot is able to keep the aircraft in a proper orientation by the use of the panel of instruments without any reference to the horizon. Pilots are trained to fly IFR by an in-flight instructor while wearing a hood to block a view of the horizon while still being able to see the instrument panel.

Pilots who are not IFR proficient and fly into bad weather where the horizon is not visible will quickly find themselves in real trouble. Within forty-five seconds they may experience what is termed spatial disorientation. This is the inability to determine the position, location, and motion of the aircraft relative to its environment. This is where the pilot's sensory interpretation of position and motion—what the pilot believes to be true—conflicts with reality. This situation develops not because a pilot does not know what the instruments are there for, but because a pilot has not been trained to rely on the reading of the instruments over their own self-perception.

Untrained pilots who lose the horizon will think they are flying straight and level when in reality they are in what is called a "death spiral," where aircraft steadily loses altitude while going in a circle before crashing into the ground. Unaware, pilots will perceive that they have control of the aircraft when in reality they don't. Without IFR training, without trust in the instrument readings, and without the discipline to compensate for their self-perception, a pilot will likely crash when there is impaired visibility.

● ● ● ● ●

This illustration represents all the principles being presented in this chapter. The bad weather is the stressor, which is analogous to inner personal turmoil or conflict. The horizon represents flawed, personal Core Beliefs which become the only point of reference. The instrument panel and the information it provides is representative of the Core Truth.

With total dependence on self-perception (the horizon, or what can be seen), the only options for the untrained and unaware pilot when the stressor (the bad weather) develops is to turn back to where the flight began, to land, to luck out that the weather quickly clears, or to crash.

The dominance that self-perception can have over reality is such an important point that we will share two real-life stories to demonstrate the significance of what we are trying to say about the relationship between truth and self-perception.

A STORY ABOUT JOHN F. KENNEDY, JR.: THE COST OF FALSE SELF-PERCEPTION

John F. Kennedy, Jr. was an accomplished, well-educated child of privilege. He was handsome, articulate, and influential as a personality and as a publisher. He possessed a great deal of personal talent. But with all of his talent, fame, and fortune, he became in a tragic way a victim of the limitations of his own self-perception.

On the evening of July 16, 1999, John, his wife, and his sister-in-law were in a single-engine aircraft owned and piloted by John. They were on their way from the Essex County Airport in New Jersey with the intention of flying along the coast of Connecticut, across Rhode Island Sound and the open ocean to Martha's Vineyard, Massachusetts. Night was falling, and a summertime haze had set in over the ocean as John left the familiar and orienting view of the lights along the shore and a fading horizon. He was unprepared for what would happen next or for a challenge that would cost him his life and the lives of two others.

John had experience as a fair-weather pilot, but he was neither trained nor certified to fly IFR. When John encountered flying conditions requiring that he solely rely on instruments rather than his own sensations, he got into trouble.

John overestimated his own ability. He thought he could depend on his self-perception, what he used when flying in fair weather, to keep his aircraft aright in zero-visibility conditions. After all, it was a short distance to the airport at Martha's Vineyard. As he went along, depending only on what he perceived to be the reality of his situation and unable to interpret the information available to him from his instruments, he flew his aircraft into the ocean.

The official report on the investigation of the crash by the National Transportation Safety Board cited ". . . the pilot's failure to maintain control of the airplane during a descent over water at night which was a result of spatial disorientation." He was overcome in his ability to distinguish up from down based strictly on his sensations.

Talent was not what John F. Kennedy, Jr. needed on the night of July 16, 1999. What he needed was the training and confidence to believe and respond to the truth, to what his instruments were telling him. He had not prepared himself to function as a pilot in difficult weather conditions, so trying to fly at night in a blinding haze—along with not being able to process the facts being presented by his instruments—he crashed the plane, killing himself and all those on the journey with him.

• • • • •

What will follow at this point is another story, but in this story self-perception was married to objective truth in such a way that an in-flight problem like the one depicted in the previous story had quite a different outcome.

A STORY ABOUT CHESLEY "SULLY" SULLENBERGER: TRUTH STARING YOU IN THE FACE

On January 15, 2009, US Airways Flight 1549 took off from LaGuardia Airport in New York City in full daylight and in good weather. The aircraft was piloted by Chesley "Sully" Sullenberger, a veteran fighter pilot who had flown commercially for twenty-nine years. He was also an experienced glider pilot and aviation safety expert. During the climb-out after takeoff, about one minute into the flight, a flock of Canada geese flew into the flight path of the aircraft. As a result, both engines were disabled by the birds being drawn into the jet's engine intakes.

Looking to his instrument panel for information about the aircraft's performance, he quickly saw that his plane had lost propulsion and could not sustain powered flight. Captain Sullenberger notified air traffic control of his situation and requested clearance to make an emergency landing. He was told he was cleared to return to LaGuardia or proceed to Teterboro Airport across the Hudson River in New Jersey.

With no engine thrust, the aircraft had essentially become a very inefficient glider. The plane was rapidly losing both speed and altitude. Studying his flight instruments and integrating this information with his considerable experience as a pilot, Captain Sullenberger judged that he could not make it to either of the nearest airports and would have to seek an alternative place to land. He chose to land, or "ditch," the aircraft with its 155 passengers and crew into the Hudson River. He radioed to air traffic control, "We can't do it, we're gonna be in the Hudson."

The aircraft made a belly landing in the waters of the Hudson River. Due to the pilot's considerable skill, the fuselage remained intact and all the passengers and crew exited onto the wings and were rescued by nearby boats. This entire ordeal from start to finish took place in just five minutes. Because of Captain Sullenberger's familiarity with and trust in his instruments and the courage to apply what he knew in overwhelmingly challenging circumstances, he accomplished what the National Transportation

Safety Board recorded in its investigation as "the most successful ditching in aviation history."

Captain Sullenberger's reading of his flight instruments let him know the truth—he would never be able, as instructed, to reach any nearby airport and would have to make an unconventional landing in the closest uninhabited area. He correctly chose the Hudson River.

• • • • •

As the two stories you have just read illustrate so well—where self-perception is educated through preparation and experience and is tempered by open-mindedness and objectivity—better decisions will be made, and, as it relates to being married, relationships will be stronger. Where self-perception is dominated by Core Beliefs forged out of psychic trauma, misinformation, or egotism, the potential for adverse life events is increased and the ability to be better at being married will be diminished.

CHAPTER 3

The Formation of Core Beliefs

As you read along, this chapter may seem like a dissertation on human development and not a chapter about being better at being married; however, the content of this chapter is very important to the purpose of this book and for you to better understand the origin of your self-perception. This chapter will help you appreciate how each developmental stage of your life has contributed to the assembly of your controlling beliefs. Completion of this chapter will increase your knowledge about the need for understanding your Core Story.

Children are intellectual and emotional sponges. They are constantly observing and recording; they are constantly learning what they like and what is safe; they are constantly learning what they don't like and what is dangerous; they are constantly experiencing what gets them into trouble and what pleases others. Many of these impressions are unconsciously translated into a controlling cluster of Core Beliefs about such important matters as safety, control, and self-esteem. This group of Core Beliefs forms the nucleus around which self-perception is developed—how we all first come to see ourselves as children and then as adults.

These Core Beliefs create a point of reference that will guide the interpretation of relational, emotional, intellectual, experiential, and spiritual matters throughout life. If these Core Beliefs are functional and developmentally appropriate, they will serve the married adult well. If these Core Beliefs were born out of trauma, misinformation, bad example, or depravity, many will likely be inadequate and dysfunctional in supporting the relational skills needed for being married.

Core Beliefs are developed and refined over three stages of life. The first stage begins early in childhood and continues until the teen years begin. The second stage continues throughout the teen years until about the age of twenty-five. The third and final stage is likely where you are today, and this stage will continue for the rest of your life.

THE INITIAL STAGE OF CORE BELIEF FORMATION

Some children are nurtured while others are not. Some grow up easily and some grow up in hardship. Some get through their teen years and enter adulthood emotionally intact and some do not. Children form patterns of thinking and behavior around what they experience; they internalize the emotional tone within their family; they obey what they are told to do; they form impressions about people and events; they accept as true what they are told by those they trust.

The problem is that children are very impressionable and as detailed observers they do not have the sophistication or aptitude to engage in critical thinking about what is happening around them. For better or worse, Core Beliefs formed during childhood will cast a psychological shadow for a lifetime. This shadow of influence will forever impact a person's self-perception. These early-formed Core Beliefs will continue to influence how people see themselves, relate to others, and function in the world at large—and will influence being married.

> *For better or worse, Core Beliefs formed during childhood will cast a psychological shadow for a lifetime.*

Childhood experiences are not always a deliberate and purposeful teacher because childhood experiences can be random and arbitrary and their impact can be unpredictable. With childhood experiences, time, place, person, intensity, and context become the teacher. Experiences can be positive, such as when a child experiences love, kindness, security, and worth. At other times negative experiences can come through such things as the death of a loved one, abuse, parental divorce, social deprivation, injury, or illness.

A child has no inventory of prior experience and only limited knowledge with which to make experiential comparisons. As a result, premature conclusions and inaccurate assessments are common. Because of their cognitive and experiential limitations, children are vulnerable to the influence of adults as to how they might interpret what is being experienced. Sometimes the insight provided by adults is helpful, and at other times adult insight may only propagate their own faulty Core Beliefs.

The associations that support a child's Core Beliefs aren't necessarily logical, valid, enlightened, or even appropriate. The Core Beliefs of a child are not always formulated or selected from among the best of alternatives. All that matters for a young child is that their system of beliefs works for them in the moment they are in. For example, a child might cope with the stress of frequent moves through dissociation—psychologically distancing themselves from reality. This is where a controlling Core Belief might develop to the effect that the only way to feel safe and secure is by not developing close friendships.

If this withdrawal behavior is perceived to work predictably to relieve the threats and stresses perceived by a child, this way of thinking will be unknowingly internalized into a Core Belief and carried into adulthood. Following this example further in time, a persistent Core Belief where relational difficulties are avoided through withdrawal is a sure starter for hardships in being married.

Staying with the example just cited, acting on a Core Belief that withdrawal is the best way to avoid relational stress may work for a child, but this approach is totally inappropriate for a married adult. Just imagine the turmoil that dissociation (distancing yourself from a demanding situation) will create when trying to work through a family problem.

Another example of faulty Core Belief formation involves children faced with crushing expectations. There might be pressure from family, peers, and from school to make good grades, to be a skilled athlete, and to run with the right crowd. In first dealing with these expectations, a child might be driven to overachieve in areas where they possess strength and aptitude in order to compensate for areas of perceived inadequacy. The pressures of expectation might become so great that cheating, fabricating excuses, or blaming others for perceived personal failures are rationalized as acceptable because they produce the desired outcome—the appearance of achievement.

A child will attempt to maintain their self-esteem by doing the things that will make them feel good about themselves and result in them being well thought of by others. Following the example just presented, whatever way of thinking supports a child achieving expected performance is the way of thinking that will be repeated. Life solutions, when habitually depended upon, will become part of a child's Core Beliefs and will be carried into adulthood. If this way of thinking has worked well in the past, why not also in the future? These belief-driven solutions may work for a child, but habits of belief may not work as well for an adult.

A child might also find themselves in a situation that demands they assume an inordinate amount of personal responsibility. A child may be the older sibling in a single parent home, or the disability of a family member may require that a child assume significant household responsibilities. When a situation of hyper-responsibility is forced upon a child, they have no choice but to accept this obligation; they are suddenly and prematurely placed in a position of control. In such a situation, responsibility and control can forever become linked in the mind of a child. In cases like this, a child could carry into adulthood a chronic tendency to believe that they are responsible to make everything all right for everyone else, even if at their own expense. A Core Lie that says assuming responsibility establishes control over a situation is a formula for emotional and physical burnout.

In a perfect world, no ill-formed, trauma-induced, totally self-serving Core Beliefs will ever survive the journey from childhood to adulthood. In a perfect world, all of the coping mechanisms supported by the Core Beliefs of a child will be modified over time through maturation. In a perfect world, the Core Beliefs of a child will refine over time as the adult acknowledges their Core Wounds and Core Lies and becomes better able to interpret and understand their own motivations and inclinations as driven by their Core Beliefs. In a perfect world, coping as an adult will rely on Core Beliefs that are aligned with age, experience, knowledge, and opportunity. In a perfect world, Core Lies will be exposed and corrected. However, it is not a perfect world.

Controlling Core Beliefs that were once adaptive and a source of stability for a child can become a major stumbling block for a person trying to function effectively and relationally in the adult world. Controlling Core Beliefs that were effective and expedient for a child can be inappropriate for the adult, especially when involved in the complexity of a marital relationship.

> *Controlling Core Beliefs that were once adaptive and a source of stability for a child can become a major stumbling block for a person trying to function effectively and relationally in the adult world.*

THE INSPECTION STAGE OF CORE BELIEF FORMATION

The period between ages thirteen and twenty-five are the pre-adult years. The early stage of childhood is over, and Core Beliefs have been programmed based upon life experience up to the teen years. The driving questions during this stage in life are, *Who am I?* and *What do I want to do with what I find out?*

The inspection stage is the period in life when the world suddenly becomes a very large place with lots of new choices, challenges, and opportunities. It is during this period that independence and self-determination are road tested. This is the time when the reality of life choices and the repercussions from relationships are unable to be shielded by parents.

This is a time of instability and insecurity because it is a time of questioning and adjusting, of letting go and latching on. This is a time when the veil comes off the eyes and some of the old ways of thinking and relating to others are found not to work well anymore. This is a point in life when decisions are made to adjust or entrench, to do some soul searching or ride it out in hopes that things will improve, to get mad about the whole thing or blame everything on somebody else, or to deny that anything needs to be done at all.

The pre-adult begins to shift their attention from being influenced toward exerting influence. A pre-adult has increased power through physical, social, intellectual, and sexual means to significantly impact others. How the pre-adult chooses to channel this newfound influence will determine the nature and quality of relationships as an adult.

Worth also takes on additional significance. Self-esteem is no longer just about what a pre-adult thinks of themselves, it's also about what others think. There is psychic tension for pre-adults when trying to maintain the integrity of their own identity, while at the same time seeking peer acceptance. This is a time for learning how to live in community, and this includes learning how to share relational time with the opposite sex. The existence of this tension between an emphasis on self and a consideration of others will need to be dealt with throughout life.

Then there is security. A pre-adult assumes risk in order to explore. There is psychological risk when pursuing an answer to the question, *Who am I?* Exploration is necessary for the pre-adult to discover if they are more than they were as a child. Will such an exploration be complete? Will there be a guide during this exploration? What will be done with what is found? Will there emerge an adult emancipated from faulty childhood Core Beliefs or merely an adult child?

Pre-adulthood is a critical time in the life-cycle of Core Belief formation. The turmoil of self-conscious questioning, which is the hallmark of the pre-adult period, is a necessary process for the timely maintenance of Core Beliefs. Core Beliefs will either be affirmed or modified as a result of this questioning. Core Beliefs can also remain unquestioned and unchanged. This self-inventory can be hard to watch and difficult to endure. If this hard but necessary developmental step is avoided or minimized, significant relational determinates that are imbedded in Core

Beliefs may be carried from childhood into adulthood without ever having been examined, challenged, modified, or discarded.

Core Beliefs that become frozen in time often will not continue to work, yet sometimes neither do the substitutes. Pre-adulthood is a period of trial and error. It is a time for a young person to determine if they will seek to be more than their past or just the extension of their past. This process of reconciliation between what someone wants and what others expect and deserve begins in pre-adulthood, but it does not end there. There will be a lifelong struggle to maintain a balance between self-interest and the best interest of others, between fact and belief, and between giving and receiving.

THE INSIGHT STAGE OF CORE BELIEF FORMATION

The adult emerges from pre-adulthood only to realize that the self-centeredness of childhood and the pre-adult search for meaningful, stable relationships have not gone away. In fact, an adult will spend the rest of their life attempting to maintain a balance between the yin and yang of what is good for the self and what is best for others. The journey into adulthood brings along Core Beliefs that were established during the childhood and pre-adult stages of life. These emotional bags will need to be unpacked and examined by the adult. Core Belief is part of the continuum of life, not an endpoint.

This story illustrates that examining and refining Core Beliefs may be required at any point in life.

A STORY FROM TERRY: IT'S NEVER TOO LATE

I was fifty-one years old when I finally identified my Core Lie. I was directing a counseling center and had just completed the doctoral program for Personality, Religion, and Culture at Boston University. I studied under the leadership of Dr. Merle Jordan whose book *Taking on the Gods* had inspired me to choose this area of study.

My dissertation centered on the power of an adult's Core Beliefs developed during childhood. My research emphasized the impact of childhood trauma on the formation of Core Beliefs and the subsequent dissociation that is often the result. Over the years of my doctoral studies and as a result of the related group experiences, I became much more familiar with my own Core Story. I was able to identify my own Core Wound: that I felt abandoned. I was also able to discover my Core Lie: that it is up to me to make everything all right. My Core Belief was that I am responsible. I came to realize that my life, my counseling, my being married were all diminished by the exhaustion brought about by over-responsibility. All of this insight came as a result of analyzing the impact of my Core Story—what I had come to believe as a high functioning adult to be true about life, work, and relationships. My Core Story revelations were included as a case study in a book by Dr. Jordan titled *Reclaiming Your Story*.

I resigned my position as director of a counseling center with sixty-four people on my waiting list. I released myself from the bondage of my Core Lie that I am responsible. Understanding my Core Story and identifying my Core Lie helped me realize how vulnerable I am to succumbing to the Messiah Complex (trying to save everyone). This knowledge has helped me to better enjoy my life, my coaching others, and my being married.

· · · · ·

The Core Beliefs of an adult should be sought out and understood because the stakes for understanding are higher for an adult. But self-understanding is not an easy process. Real understanding requires a mix of courage, humility, curiosity, patience, forgiveness, and correct information. To gain understanding takes a deliberate effort.

Unlike children and pre-adults, the life of an adult can have a significant impact on the lives of many others, especially children. But adulthood may be the first time that many people have been forced—because of personal or relational failure—to sort out and understand the residue of Core Beliefs carried over from their childhood and the pre-adult years. Adulthood is a time for identifying alternatives in life that were not known or felt to be possible previously.

Being stuck in what is happening, rather than focusing on why things are happening, can cause adults to find themselves losing their sense of peace, their effectiveness with others, and their enjoyment of life. Blocked by a lack of courage to address their difficulties and the absence of resolve to go beyond themselves for answers, adults can suffer personally and end up damaging their relationships.

Questioning part of one's self with the possibility for change to occur, no matter how gently this is done or how necessary it may be, takes both courage and faith. Courage is required to admit that in some way you are incomplete. Faith involves accepting as truth something that is outside of your own ability and experience—and substituting this truth for something that is critical to your life. Exercising faith is spiritual work. Spiritual exploration is what opens up the possibility for personal and relational growth.

> *Questioning part of one's self with the possibility for change to occur, no matter how gently this is done or how necessary it may be, takes both courage and faith.*

The spiritual consideration involves evaluating what is coming in, what is going out, and what is going on in our lives. This is the dimension of personality where we seek to integrate the physical, mental, social, and emotional aspects of life into a meaningful whole. This is the aspect of our being where we discover through our own personal search that there is information beneficial to our life that lies outside of our own experience and consciousness. Making use of this new information is an act of faith, thus it is a spiritual endeavor. This new information will replace the previous learning and interpretations that have been depended upon in the past but experienced to be incorrect, incomplete, and problematic.

Consider this verse composed by Terry.

Waken to the Unseen World

There is a secret life that brings joy,
it is something you can taste and experience.
It is a hidden place that longs to be found

> by all those who seek.
> To those who are broken
> light comes in the darkness.
> Hope is revealed to the hopeless
> with a compassionate touch.
> The human heart is greater
> and larger than any pain.
> It is made real in suffering.
> I am a witness.
> You can overcome.
> This certain reality comes to those who ask
> expecting to find an answer.

Developing yourself spiritually will take humility, courage, and discipline. It will take humility to admit that there are truths you have yet to learn and that the answers you seek to the questions and dilemmas of your life lie beyond your own knowledge, experience, and capabilities. It will take courage to trust that new information you did not create is sufficient to replace your thoughts about important things that you have held to be true for a long time. It will take discipline to overcome the pain of change and to be sure that your sources for information are examined closely and proven in their reliability.

So many of the impressions of life formed in early and middle childhood are a result of what has been seen and experienced. The adult discovers that this is not enough, that what they have seen and experienced is often incomplete. The last stone in the foundation of a good life is allowing faith to introduce possibilities to you that were previously unknown.

You may have already come to realize that truth is not dependent on your ability to know. It may be the affirmation of a trusted friend, the writing of a knowledgeable author, or the tenets of a religious community, but in one way or another you will find value in opening yourself up to considering the knowledge and experience of others.

CHAPTER 4

The Power of Core Beliefs

Core Beliefs are personal and powerful. They are absent conscious awareness in their influence. They rule over your self-perception. They determine how you feel about yourself and what you will do to protect and assert your perceived self-interest. They will determine how well you will function in being married and how you will choose to raise your children.

Core Beliefs are more feeling than knowing. Core Beliefs are hard to change because of your emotional attachment to them, and they can work for your benefit or to your detriment.

Core Beliefs are not always rational or even factual as they are set in your mind while still a young child. Core Beliefs are primal and early formed as they involve what you believed was necessary to survive and thrive. They dominate over all other beliefs because they involve such critical matters as maintaining control over your circumstances, being valued by others, and keeping yourself from harm.

One of the objectives of this book is to establish that there is truth beyond your own experience, that Core Beliefs can be identified, examined, and educated, and that some of your Core Beliefs actually may be Core Lies—perhaps arising from Core Wounds. The challenge for us is to convince you it is worth the effort to learn what really makes you tick, so that you may then become more self-aware and thus better at living life.

We will try very hard not to inject personal prejudice into what is intended to be an open, transparent presentation of information that will assist you in your journey of self-discovery and self-help. When referring to the Bible, our intent is to merely endorse it as a reliable and time-tested source of information about every aspect of life.

It is through the influence of Core Beliefs that each of us defines ourselves and establishes our view of reality—our self-perception. We each take what we see and what we are told and process this information through a private system of belief-based interpretation. Much like an optical lens alters the course of a beam of light, Core Beliefs will bend the rays of reality to create an image that looks like our self-perception.

THE EXTERNAL WORLD

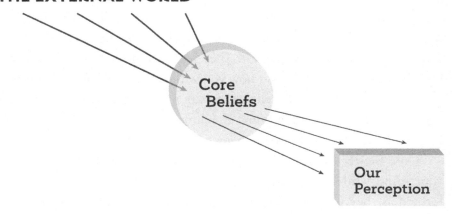

Belief is a powerful and determinate force within each of our lives because what we believe becomes our truth, regardless of facts. Our Core Beliefs will dictate how we think, feel, and act. So if your goal is to remove barriers in being married, you must improve awareness of your Core Beliefs and Core Lies. They are highly influential in determining how you think and behave.

Beliefs affect your ability to relate to what is going on in the moment, your ability to distinguish fact from fiction, and your ability to distinguish between your own needs and the needs of others.

What you believe has consequences, especially when considering the constant proximity and high relational expectations associated with being married. Beliefs affect your ability to relate to what is going on in the moment, your ability to distinguish fact from fiction, and your ability to distinguish between your own needs and the needs of others. Beliefs color your objectivity and critical thinking. Beliefs allow you to either be present in the moment, connected, and appropriately responsive, or your beliefs can cause you to be stuck in the bubble of a self-synthesized world. Consider the following illustration.

AN ILLUSTRATION: CONFLICTING CORE BELIEFS AND BEING MARRIED

Raising children is one of the most important things that a married couple has in common. After all, it takes a contribution of genes from both parents to make a child in the first place! This is one matter where everyone needs to be on the same page.

But partnering in parenting can have its rough spots. One reason for this is that the Core Beliefs formed by a mom and dad out of the emotional environment in which they were raised may be very different in their expression. For instance, maybe a dad holds a Core Belief that self-esteem is established through high performance. He was raised in a household where the prevailing point of view was that you should be ashamed if you are not an achiever. Passing on what he experienced in his home, this dad believes that pressure enhances performance.

Perhaps the mom is all for the children doing well at school and in sports. On this point she and her husband agree. She is accomplished herself, but the Core Belief emanating from the years with her parents is that self-esteem should be based upon authenticity and personal integrity. She has high expectations for the children, but her approach of mentoring for motivation is in stark contrast to her husband's press for success. So when her husband pressures the children about grades, demands fewer mistakes, and wants to see better performance at games, they begin to disagree and criticize one another's approach to parenting.

Something has to change if there is to be any peace between mom and dad! Both parents sincerely believe they are doing the best for their children.

It is likely that neither the mom nor the dad in this example have thought about developing a mutually agreeable parenting plan that addresses the actual needs of their children. It is unlikely that they are consciously aware of the Core Beliefs that are influencing their respective views about responsible parenting.

The solution to this marital impasse will not be found in a win for dad and a loss for mom. What is needed is the mutual development of and support for an approach to parenting that is not rooted in the parent's past but is actually fitted to their children's personalities, their individual aptitudes, and the opportunities available to them.

• • • • •

The purpose of this book is not to suggest what you should believe, but to encourage you to seek out the truth from any credible source about how you are living your life. What you believe about power and control, about affection and esteem, and about safety and security have a tremendous influence on how you live out your daily life, how you function being married, and how you raise your children. It is important for you to get in touch with these beliefs because they determine how you are able to relate to others and function in your daily life.

The Core Beliefs that define your self-perception—beliefs about safety, predictability, and dignity—determine whether your emotional energy is focused on learning and adapting or on protecting and entrenching, on reaching out or on pulling away, on building up or on tearing down. We hope what is being presented will create a platform for conversation—first within yourself and then with others—about the power of Core Beliefs, your need to learn what they are, the long-lasting emotional impact of a Core Wound, the relational danger presented by a Core Lie, and ways to internalize Core Truths.

Core Lies may remain as a residue, even after they have been identified and replaced with Core Truths. Core Lies will not be forgotten, but hopefully they will be neutralized in their influence because of better insight and information. They will always try to butt in while you are thinking.

Once alerted, you can choose how you want to think and act. You can identify the Core Wound and the resultant Core Lie, and you can choose the Core Truth over a Core Lie.

Like so many of us, you may be defensive about taking a deep dive into what causes you to think and act the way you do. No one wants to hear that their behavior is hurtful to their spouse or disruptive to being married. Focused and intensive self-examination is difficult because it is hard to do and can be threatening to your self-perception. We merely want to open up the possibility in your mind that a thorough, purposeful self-examination of what you believe deep down can ultimately be helpful. We will help you in this process of self-discovery using the Core Story approach detailed in Section 2.

Maybe this book will open up the possibility in your mind that what others know or what others may see about you can help you improve the way you live your life. This involvement of others whom you voluntarily bring into your circle can prove helpful, not because others are better or smarter than you, but simply because they can offer other perspectives for you to consider on your journey toward a more truth-based self-awareness.

Everyone wants to think that their controlling Core Beliefs are intellectually and morally sound. Many of them are, but some may not be. Intellectually, we all want to feel that our behavior is good for us. Morally, we want to feel that our behavior is not harmful to anyone else. This perception may be a self-serving rationalization rather than a reality, but, nevertheless, this is how most of us want to feel. Beliefs that are felt to be intellectually and morally sound are thus presumed to be valid. If presumed to be valid, we justify holding onto our Core Beliefs—unexplored and unaltered—because of their assumed legitimacy.

Let us make clear this point: Core Beliefs will not necessarily cause problems just because they were formed as children or because they are not totally correct. If your life is going well, if your problems at home are manageable, if your relationship with your spouse is intact despite some challenges, you have no incentive beyond your curiosity to spend a lot of time and effort searching out your Core Beliefs. You won't need to climb a tree just to get some shade! However, if you seem to be making yourself uncomfortable, if relationships are being strained, and decisions are making things worse instead of better, you will benefit from an inventory of your most influential Core Beliefs and being on the lookout for the Core Wounds and Core Lies.

Seeking out and understanding your Core Beliefs is not only important for the sake of the health of your relationships but for your own mental health. Self-perception as shaped by Core Beliefs can act like a double-edged sword that can cut in either of two directions. Cutting in one direction, Core Beliefs that are dysfunctional, misinformed, or immature can cause your perception and judgment to be faulty. Cutting the other way, when your Core Beliefs create expectations that you cannot meet for yourself, you can turn inward and experience harsh self-judgment and self-loathing. Either way, if Core Beliefs emanate from a Core Wound or constitute a Core Lie, they can provoke attitudes and behaviors that are harmful to being married. Whatever way the sword of self-perception swings, misplaced feelings, unrealistic expectations, and inappropriate actions can adversely affect being married either because of your unhappiness or the unhappiness you are causing for your spouse.

Core Beliefs become your judge and jury. Self-judgment can be as harsh as criticism coming from someone else. You may be living your life at the mercy of underdeveloped Core Beliefs or at the mercy of Core Lies formed out of a Core Wound experienced when you were only a child.

What if one of your Core Beliefs is that you are not good enough? Might this self-perception be driving you to work too much in order to prove yourself, only to end up being away from your family too much? Could this notion about self-worth have been created in your mind because you could never please your overbearing father? Would your life be better if you became aware of this Core Lie, challenged it, and replaced it with a Core Truth about yourself?

What if one of your Core Beliefs is that you are undesirable? Might this self-perception be the reason you are hyper-concerned about your appearance, where you live, and the car you drive? Might these beliefs be the reason you have too much debt from spending too much maintaining a lavish lifestyle? Could these beliefs about being unattractive have come out of a childhood Core Wound created by poverty? Would your life and being married be better if the strain brought about by considerable debt was lessened because you became aware of this Core Lie and replaced it with a Core Truth about yourself?

What if your Core Belief is that you are expendable? Might this self-perception be the reason that you are so possessive of your spouse, untrusting, and jealous? Could this Core Belief have risen out of the Core Wound created by your early childhood separation due to your parents' divorce and your feeling of being left behind? Would your life be better, would you improve your relationship with your spouse, if you became aware of this Core Lie and replaced it with the Core Truth about yourself? Even with the help of others and all the evidence in the world, you are the only one who can choose what the Core Truths are for your life.

When trying to get yourself out of an emotional or relational pit, you will need three things—time, safety, and good information. First, taking time both mitigates the ravages of urgency and creates room for learning and interpretation. Taking time forces you to be patient and wait. Time provides the opportunity for gathering, thinking, and trying.

Second, safety is not literally a place, but a state of mind. Safety is when you drop your defensiveness, suspend a rush to judgment, and give yourself permission to consider new information and new possibilities. This is an environment where you can venture into the spiritual aspects of your personality, the place where you assign relevance and significance to what is believed and what is being thought about. This is the space that gives you room to consider whether to live your life based on what is or on what could be, whether to live a life based on trust or on fear.

Third, good information needs to be your diet during this time of searching and contemplation. Working within the haven provided by time and safety, you can enter into a period of honest inquiry. You can search out your own story using tools like the Core Story process detailed in

Section 2. Based upon what you discover about yourself, you can seek out what others have to offer regarding the matters that are of concern to you.

Belief is established when experience and learning make an impression that is internalized as truth. To give up or change a way of thinking is to ask ourselves to alter Core Beliefs about such vital matters as what gives us and others value, makes us influential, and keeps us secure. Breaking the bond of a Core Belief involves the intense interaction between the mental, emotional, and spiritual dimensions of the personality.

Breaking the bond of a Core Belief involves the intense interaction between the mental, emotional, and spiritual dimensions of the personality.

What follows is a real-life story about the necessity for spiritual work to be performed to correct a spiritual problem.

A STORY: THIS IS A SPIRITUAL PROBLEM

Larry was born to fly. He sought risk and speed. Flying made him feel alive. By the age of fifteen he had completed his first solo flight. Larry had his commercial license by age nineteen and had a college degree in aeronautics at age twenty-one. He was a top of the class Naval aviator at age twenty-three and was Grumman A-6 Intruder Jet Bomber qualified by age twenty-four.

Larry was a combat pilot during the Vietnam War. He flew regular sorties to drop 14,000-pound bomb loads on enemy combatants. He received a Navy Commendation Medal that read, "For heroic achievement as pilot of a jet aircraft . . . ." Yet, he voluntarily and abruptly quit flying upon his final landing on the aircraft carrier, USS Enterprise.

Larry turned in his wings and shed his hard-earned identity as a jet pilot for reasons he did not understand. He simply could not continue his combat missions. Physically, Larry stayed well-conditioned; mentally, he maintained a high level of training, completed his missions as planned, and trained other pilots; socially, he was faithful in being married and remained in good standing with the Navy; emotionally, Larry had become unsettled about his wartime role.

In the years after leaving the Navy, Larry's life was full. He had a good marriage, children, and a great job. He drove a Porsche and had a ski boat in the garage. Yet, with all this he was still depressed and in turmoil. As he came to realize later, young war combatants are well-trained in their physical, mental, and social roles and are "steeled up" emotionally for warfare, but the moral and spiritual consequences of their service in war are not experienced until much later.

Larry sought professional help. The psychotherapist asked Larry, "What did you do in the military?" After his reply the therapist then asked, "Did you kill anyone?"

Larry was stunned, even angered by the question, but he answered, "Yes." The therapist did not miss the angst in Larry's response.

Larry was asked to come back in a week with an estimate of how many people he may have killed in combat. When Larry returned he dumped 400 pennies on a table, one for each person he may have killed. He was then challenged with this question to be answered at the next session, "What right do you think you had to do what you did?" The therapist went on to say, "Don't tell me what the Navy told you; tell me your thoughts."

When Larry returned to the therapist, he said, "I feel I have a right to kill someone if they are trying to kill me or a member of my family, or if they are trying to take away my freedom." He then added, "The problem is that none of these conditions existed for me."

Based upon Larry's reply to the question, the psychotherapist said, "I can't help you. You have a spiritual problem, not a psychological one." This very honest and insightful observation opened a door for Larry to walk through and enter into the spiritual dimension of his personality.

Larry used his mind and summoned his courage just as he had done while training as a jet pilot. Larry's level of spiritual development was not enough to allow him to mediate the conflict between the intellectual and emotional dimensions of his personality. He needed a standard against which to evaluate and resolve his crisis of conscience.

He discovered unexamined and untreated wounds of conscience. He felt that he had bloody hands; he felt his soul was seared by moral injury. He set out on a spiritual journey to search for forgiveness and inner peace. Larry was handicapped to some extent by his previous experiences with church and religious people, but nevertheless he acknowledged that he had a big spiritual challenge ahead and was in need of help finding his way.

Larry began his journey into spiritual reconstruction and found healing and identity re-formation through prayer, bible study, and the acceptance of the "come to me" offer of Jesus Christ. Larry established the balance in his life, the full build-out of his personality, that had been missing for too long.

· · · · ·

Faith and spirituality are not synonymous with religion, and we are not using these terms in a religious context. The alteration of belief is not in and of itself a religious endeavor and does not require a religious experience. Belief and faith and spirituality are part of the human experience, regardless of any religious involvement. The importance of doing spiritual work, of looking deep inside ourselves, of searching for such things as meaning, significance, and forgiveness, is a similar quest for all people, regardless of their theological bent.

> *Belief and faith and spirituality are part of the human experience, regardless of any religious involvement.*

Faith supported by courage and backed by hope and trust will be necessary to break the hold that a Core Lie may have upon your life. Accepting as truth something that is outside of your own ability and experience—and substituting this truth for something that is a major component of your self-perception—takes faith. At its core, faith is the acceptance of truth without proof, but that truth is confirmed when it is experienced as being trustworthy.

The process of self-inquiry is intense and emotional. It can be internally confrontational. Where self-perception holds you captive to your existing Core Beliefs, spiritual exploration is the only thing that will open the possibility for personal and relational growth.

Even though belief touches all aspects of our lives, strangely enough we are not always aware of all that we believe. Some belief is conscious. Sometimes this conscious belief is evident to others through our behavior, and sometimes it is not. Other beliefs are absent from our conscious awareness in that we do not perceive their influence. Sometimes others can see the evidence of these beliefs in our behavior and sometimes they cannot. Whether conscious or outside of our awareness, all beliefs must be sought out and subjected to a spiritual inventory. When we fully engage our spiritual side, personal defensiveness will be suspended in a courageous act of seeking out what is really true for our life and time.

What may come about through your self-inquiry is that parts of your self-perception as formed through your Core Beliefs are flawed in some way. A need for self-inquiry may be provoked by a crisis of conscience. It may come from a dilemma in being married or a failure at work. It may be brought about by the collapse of a relationship or some public disgrace. When you get stuck, when you shut down or are shut out, it should motivate you to examine your Core Beliefs in search for the Core Lie with a commitment to replace it with the time-tested and trustworthy information—the Core Truth.

Core Lies are often exposed as being ineffective in times of personal crisis. This exposure is the constructive side of problems. Times of crisis are when you are in the greatest need for your best thinking, yet it is a time when you may be least open to engaging in a lengthy self-analysis.

The devil we know often seems better than the devil we don't know! Giving unquestioned leeway to your self-perception, and thus to your Core Beliefs, in times of crisis is fine as long as your thinking is clear and your actions are appropriate. You don't want faulty beliefs to be unintentionally sabotaging your own problem-solving efforts.

CHAPTER 5

Terry's Life Story

All of the information presented to you so far has been for the purpose of preparing you to better understand the deep personal meaning that can come from shining a light on your Core Beliefs through storytelling and story-based self-discovery. Now that you are equipped with the basic concepts of how Core Beliefs are formed and how influential these Core Beliefs can be, we want you to read the life story of one of the authors, Terry S. Smith.

Using what you have already learned, you will be able to read this chapter and anticipate, based upon your own analysis, what will be presented about Terry's story in Chapter 6, titled *Understanding Terry's Life Story as a Core Story*. The concepts you have learned will create a context for you to see the situational and developmental elements in this story and attach practical meaning to what you read in Chapters 1–4.

We believe that by reading a real-life story and seeing how Core Wounds and Core Lies originate and can be replaced with Core Truth, you will better appreciate how the Core Story process (Section 2) can help you discover and understand your own Core Beliefs and how they might impact being married.

Terry's Story begins. My on-campus work at the state university was going great, even though I had intended to begin my career in the military. The war in Vietnam was still underway when I completed my Master of Theology degree in the spring of 1968, and I wanted to enlist in the military as a chaplain. It had never appealed to me to be a traditional minister in a local church. Besides, the idea of having a military officer's rank of captain fed my ego and sounded pretty good to me. The wheels of government turn slowly, though, so a new baby and a job offer to work with students at Memphis State University (now the University of Memphis) directed my career path away from the military toward teaching and counseling. This was in 1969, and today I have been teaching, counseling, and serving as a Life Coach for more than fifty years.

In the fall of 1969 my classes were full. Students were asking the same life questions I was asking. They were in rebellion against the establishment, racism, the war, and they were being confronted with all the excesses of a sexual revolution. The moral and sexual boundaries were blurred, and young people were sick of the hypocrisy they were experiencing all around them.

My work was expanding. The group I was leading hosted a seminar in the spring that would attract as many as 1,500 people from all over the southeast. We collected over 1,600,000 Betty Crocker coupons so that General Mills would buy a kidney dialysis machine for a local student with renal failure. We even helped pass legislation in Tennessee to have organ donation information placed on driver's licenses. I was experiencing success in my work. I certainly felt blessed because my achievements were far beyond what I could have ever dreamed.

Trouble begins. In the spring of 1971, my wife called me at work very upset. Shocked and concerned, I immediately went home to be with her and my two small daughters. My quick and sincere response seemed to calm things down. At the end of the semester, with my sister taking care of the girls, we took a trip so we could mend our fences and recommit to the "for better or for worse" part of our wedding vows. While on the trip I asked what I could do to make things better, and my wife replied, "Be home for supper and help put the girls to bed in the evening." I agreed to be more available to our family. I really tried to work on not being over-committed to my job and to maintaining a balance between work and home.

Then trouble reared its ugly head again. In 1973 I was tempted to commit adultery with an older woman, who was a friend of my mother. I was shocked by my own desire for the affair. Emotionally, I felt powerless because of my overwhelming feelings to honor what I professed to believe. I thought, *This must be what it was like when my alcoholic mother and father needed a drink. They would do anything, forsake anyone in order to drink. I'm going to turn out just like my parents, and my words to the students will be empty lies.* This thought scared me to death, or better put, it scared me to life.

I left my office and went immediately to confess my lustful intentions to a friend and associate. I also confessed my dark side to a Christian friend who had become the mother I never had. I told my wife about my feelings. Everyone received me with love and compassion. The lustful desires of my youth had returned. I was now married, a teacher, and a campus minister. I knew better. What was I thinking?

I told my wife that my unwholesome thoughts had nothing to do with any inadequacy on her part. She was a gracious and loving woman. I told her the problem was within me, and that I needed her help and compassionate friendship. I said that I needed to be able to honestly share with her when temptations come. Our communication did improve. We read books, went to enrichment events, sought counsel, and continued to talk. Out of this experience we cultivated a vision that has guided us, kept us together, and kept us growing in our love for one another for fifty-five years.

Trouble continues. In 1979, after ten years working on college campuses, my family and I moved to Burlington, Massachusetts. I was directing Resources for Life, a program in metropolitan Boston designed to reach out to those abused by religion and to encourage them to do their own thinking so they could feel good about their faith experience. But once again, my tendency toward over-commitment reasserted itself. I felt a responsibility to save the world, so in merely two years I was already burned out in my new work. I made a decision to live as a Christian at the age of nineteen, and this was the first time in twenty years I had simply run out of spiritual energy. At this point, I lacked passion, drive, and vision.

The family and I took off for six weeks to visit and regroup in my wife's home state of New Mexico. This trip became a milestone in my journey toward personal spiritual discovery and recovery because it was during this trip that I began an intentional process of trying to discover and expose who I really was. I asked myself the hard questions of *Who am I?* and *What do I want?* In the quietness of the open spaces in the semi-desert, thoughts came to me about what I really wanted out of life.

I even asked my children how they experienced me, and their unanimous response was, "You are too intense!"

"What can I do?" I asked.

"Lighten up," they said. This was easier said than done.

For the next three years after this self-examination in New Mexico I awakened each morning more committed than ever to seeking insight into my own thoughts. But no particular insight or inspiration came from my efforts. My spiritual mentor, Jim Woodroof, and his wife, Louine, saw my distress and chose to join my family and me in New England. But I found no relief from the internal heaviness I was experiencing. Something was wrong on the inside, and I didn't know what it was.

I had knowledge and commitment, but no joy and peace, even after the birth of our fourth daughter in 1983. Once again my family and I sought the refuge of a vacation spot in New Hampshire. I rested, enjoyed the family, studied, and read a book by Angus I. Kinnear titled *Against the Tide: A Story of Watchman Nee.* Yet, I was no closer to understanding how I felt than before I went on the trip. What I did discover was how I felt did not align with what I knew. What I knew about life, spiritual truth, and people's behavior did not seem to be helping me feel any better about myself and the work that I was attempting to do. What I knew to be true did not seem to be as influential as what went on unseen and unconsciously within my own mind. I realized that I didn't fully understand what I was feeling, where my feelings were coming from, or why I was feeling the way I did.

Awareness emerges. I began teaching a Sunday morning Bible class at a church in Burlington. In preparing to teach lessons out of the New

Testament Gospel of John, I kept thinking about the book about Watchman Nee. I recalled a story in the book that likened a new Christian to a little boy learning to ride a bicycle. As he told the story, the little boy went through a series of rides attempting to stay erect on the bicycle only to fall over time after time. Finally, after numerous tries and the steadying support of others, the little boy prevailed in his attempt to balance on the bicycle without being supported by others.

I thought to myself: *But I'm not a new Christian. I don't think I am falling off the metaphorical bicycle of faith. Why do I keep thinking about this book?* It suddenly came to me as clear as day. *I know how to ride a bicycle, but I can't stay up because of the load I am pulling. I've hooked a wagon to my bicycle, and I have put so many people in the wagon that I can't pull the weight without falling over.* It dawned on me that instead of learning from my falls like the little boy in the story in Kinnear's book, I felt guilty for not being able to pull the load I had attached to the bicycle of my life.

Without fanfare, bright lights appearing, the appearance of fire, or the urge to otherwise shout or make wise proclamations, I heard a still, quiet voice inside of me say, "Why don't you bust the hitch to your wagon and quit trying to pull so many along with you?" This was a powerful moment for me. I knew I would need to act, and that I would need to make some personal changes. I recognized the return of my old nemeses—over-commitment and over-responsibility. I realized that I had not learned from my past and that I still wasn't able to overrule the internal message from some source within me that kept disrupting my best efforts to do right by myself, my family, my work, and others. I was trying so hard to do good for others, but I was instead imposing myself and smothering them with my involvement. I didn't understand this paradox in my life, but I knew I needed to make some changes. Like a rosebush, I knew that it would take a severe pruning, a cutting back, before I could bloom again.

Working really hard. I began my doctoral studies at Boston University in the fall of 1988. For five years I studied personality, religion, and culture under the direction of Dr. Merle Jordan. I had read his book *Taking on the Gods,* and I wanted to study under him in order to better understand how core concepts that formed so early within my family of origin were so determinate to my behavior as an adult. After studying at the Washington School of Psychiatry in 1989, I finished my doctorate in 1993, with an emphasis on the study of personality and the use of psychodrama in psychological and spiritual healing.

During the course of my doctoral studies I moved my family to Arkansas. I accepted a position as the director of a Family Life and Resource Counseling Center. I had set out in a new direction. I was out of the doldrums of my spiritual drought, and I was ready to once again begin to make a difference in the lives of others who were hurting and who were being hurt by others. At this point in my life I felt stronger, better equipped, and more ready for a new challenge than I had been in a long time. I was back in familiar territory where I was among people I knew and loved. I felt older and wiser. I had a renewed energy for the tasks that lie ahead.

I was so enthusiastic about the possibilities before me that I actually took on what was the equivalent of two jobs. As director of the counseling center, I developed a program where the emphasis was on prevention and enrichment as well as on providing counseling services. I made extensive use of groups in order to build community for my clients so that meaningful relationships could augment the counseling services that I was providing. I allied myself with a couple who were experts in the use of psychodrama as a tool for therapy, and in so doing I was introduced to people who were hurting and who would never come to a church building for help. I saw the success of this approach in creating a safe and accepting place where people could discover themselves and be honest with others about their self-discoveries.

The counseling center was part of a church of about 2,000 members. About two-thirds of the membership was made up of college students. My additional task was to help the congregation develop community. I asked couples and individuals who were interested in helping me to enter a training session. My plan was for the group to meet for three hours each Monday evening for fourteen weeks, but we ended up meeting for two and a half years. It seemed that the only thing that I was overlooking was the wagon I was once again pulling behind my bicycle. I thought I had learned my lesson about taking on more responsibility than I was assigned; I thought I had learned my lesson about taking on more responsibility than I was capable of handling. Once again, I was about to experience failure.

Searching for my story. The church board was not pleased with my work. The energy that I had expended on the Monday night sessions did not meet the expectations of the church's leadership, and they were becoming more uncomfortable with my work with unchurched people in the community. My counseling responsibilities had also become overwhelming as I accumulated sixty-four people on my waiting list to be seen at the Center. I was under a deadline to complete my doctoral dissertation, yet I seemed determined to broaden the inner circle of our family by increasing the number of people for whom I wanted to assume responsibility. My wife once again was at the end of her emotional rope and felt that I was failing to be effective at work, at home, and at church. I was working hard and felt like I knew more than ever. I was getting up early every day to read and pray and plan for serving others the best I knew how. But something was wrong, and I didn't know what.

As I looked back on my life, I could see the accumulation of over-commitment, over-responsibility, burn out, and loss of focus. I saw the toll that had been exacted in the effectiveness of my work and the quality of my life. Identifying my weaknesses—being sorry, studying, and trying harder—had so far only resulted in quickening me to my faults rather than providing the insight I needed to make meaningful changes in my life. The patterns of my life just seemed to be repeating time after time. I was very relational, but not very methodical. I always seemed to start projects with great enthusiasm but was unable to stay on task because of my tendency to get caught up in the problems of those with whom I was working. What was I missing about myself?

I spent years preparing and learning. I had two master's degrees and a doctorate. What else was there for me to know that could keep me out of these episodes of stress, failure, and disappointment? Thinking back upon my work with Dr. Jordan, it occurred to me that the problem may not exist with what I know, but with what I believe. My problem may not be in what I know I believe, but with belief of which I am unaware. *What about Core Beliefs outside of my conscious awareness that were formed early in my family of origin? Could they still be ruling my ways of thinking as an adult? Did I really know my own story? Had I really laid hold to the idea that I am more influenced by what I believe than by what I know? Have I been so intent on becoming informed that I failed to be transformed by what I learned?* I really began in earnest to search my own story for the markers that might help me identify my Core Wounds, my Core Lies, and prepare me to receive and live out of Core Truths.

> *It occurred to me that the problem may not exist with what I know, but with what I believe.*

I began by asking myself the question, "What is my ruling belief?" I pulled out my pen and wrote the following statement, "I believe that I am responsible for the well-being of others, and if I can't help them I am responsible to see that they receive the help they need." I looked at what I had written and asked myself, *Where did this come from?* My memory flashed back to when I was eight years old and my thoughts of *Poor daddy, I must take care of daddy.* I wanted to explore my story again, more deliberately, and in more depth.

Three days later I wrote a letter of resignation as the Director of the Family Life and Resource Counseling Center.

CHAPTER 6

Understanding Terry's Life Story as a Core Story

In the last chapter you read Terry's life story. No doubt based upon what you learned from reading Chapters 1–4 you saw how some of his experiences and impressions growing up might have developed into Core Beliefs that would cause personal and relational trouble for Terry as an adult. By Terry's own account in telling his story, he did indeed experience difficulties as an adult with what he was thinking, in how he carried out his work, and how he related to his wife.

Our intention is that you will be able to relate to Terry's journey of self-discovery and see what you might experience as you conduct your own Core Story exercise. We hope you will see that exploring Core Beliefs is a constructive and informative way to get at the root of self-perceptions that may feed your personal and relational difficulties in life and in being married.

My Core Story discovery begins. I began to explore my own Core Beliefs through the use of the genogram. This is a family systems model that was introduced to the mental health field in the 1940s by Dr. Murray Bowen. I used this model as a tool for therapy during my doctoral studies with Dr. Jordan. Over the years I have modified and refined this process to become what I now call the Core Story.

I knew that this tool could be helpful to me in identifying the Core Beliefs that I first developed as a child to help me feel safe, gain significance, maintain control, and influence others. I knew my Core Beliefs were layered deeply beyond my conscious awareness, and it was time for me to seek out and confront the toxic power that some of my Core Lies held over me.

I really felt that working through my Core Story might help me discover any immature and ill-formed Core Beliefs, Core Wounds, and Core Lies that could be causing me to repeat cycles of over-achievement, over-responsibility, and failure. I couldn't help recalling a quote from Dr. David Seamands stating, "Children are the world's best recorders and the world's worst interpreters." I had a very difficult childhood, so I thought maybe some of my problems as an adult were coming from the effect of flawed Core Beliefs and adverse childhood experiences. I began reconstructing my story using the approach outlined in Section 2. I knew that my Core Beliefs began forming at the point of my earliest memories, so I began to reconstruct my story from a combination of what I remembered and what I had been told.

> "Children are the world's best recorders and the world's worst interpreters."
> – Dr. David Seamands

My earliest years were full of love and care. In 1940, my mother became a child bride at the age of sixteen. She was smart and humorous and spoiled. The two grandmothers bought my parents a house when they married. This was a big help to them setting up housekeeping, but it also enabled them both to continue to act like adolescents. My dad and mom were both immature and fun-loving. They partied with their friends, and our home was a center of activity for our family. By the fourth year of being married, they had three children with a fourth to come soon after.

My parents both came from backgrounds where boundaries were very unclear. My mother was raised along with her two brothers by an alcoholic father who never told her no. Because of his alcoholism and gambling, my grandfather lost his business, resulting in my grandmother taking in boarders to make ends meet. My grandfather died when my mother was fifteen.

My father was raised by a doting mother and an uninvolved stepfather. His birth father died when he was only two years old. My grandmother was a strong, kind, loving person who spent her childhood in an orphanage. She was the religious influence on my father's life, but he had no strong and positive male role model as he and his stepfather were never close.

In 1944, my dad joined the Navy. This along with the birth of the third child threw my mother into a deep depression. She suffered a nervous breakdown and revealed to our neighbors her desire to kill all three of her children. It was during this period of my life that the Roseberry family became very important to me and my family. They lived across the street, and we always seemed to be together. They paid me a great deal of attention, and the older boys in the family taught me how to play ball, fight, sing, and just have a good time. I was not aware of my mother's problems at the time, and these were really good years in my memory mainly because of the Roseberry family. My memories of my mother are mostly of a woman preoccupied with other things. I can still remember the night when I was five years old when she dropped me, my brother, and my sister off at the movies and forgot to pick us up.

Life suddenly became very chaotic. A turning point in my parents' relationship came in 1947. In reaction to my father's philandering, my mother had an affair with my father's best friend. This was a "family secret" until I found out eighteen years later, when I was twenty-seven and my mother was forty-five years old. This was the beginning of the collapse of my family and my separation from the neighboring family who had nurtured me so well during my first years of life.

My father resented the Roseberry family because of their support of my mother, so he moved us to maintain distance from them. He forbade us from having any contact with this family or even to make mention of them in our home. This loss was very upsetting to me, not to mention coming home from school to find my mother sitting on the couch drinking wine with the washing machine repairman. I remember climbing the big tree in our yard after seeing this and feeling sick to my stomach. I felt disconnected from everything around me. I began to dissociate as a self-defense. This was the initial blow in creating a Core Wound of abandonment that would worsen over time.

When I was in the third grade, we moved again, this time to Clarksdale, Mississippi, where my father was working as an electronic field engineer for the Burroughs Corporation. My life—and our family—was in chaos. There was drinking and arguing. There was constant tension and conflict in my home as my mother used alcohol to medicate her pain. The threats and cursing finally ended in the divorce of my parents. My mother was so impaired that my father was given custody of all his children.

My brothers and sister were divided among my father's relatives while I remained with my father. For the next eighteen years, I would have no contact with my mother except once when she returned and tried to take my three-year-old brother, Robert, with her. When my dad told her to leave, I remember her getting on top of his 1949 Ford and cursing at him. She was an alcoholic, tried to commit suicide multiple times, and ended up marrying five different men. For most of my childhood years, it was just my dad and me. This situation was another blow that deepened my Core Wound of abandonment and became the basis for the Core Lie that I was alone.

My life became one move after another. I changed schools every year between the first and the seventh grade. After my parents' divorce, I lived in the home of my father's cousin or in boarding houses with my dad. On many weekends we would drive to Memphis to see my brothers and sister who were staying with relatives. We would stay with my dad's mother.

I loved those trips to Memphis. On the Sundays we were there, my grandmother would take all of us to church. My dad wanted us all to go to church, but church was not a priority for him. He had gone to church only to please his mother and was quite open with his opinion that churches were full of hypocrites. But my dad was a kind and affirming presence to me, though we seldom talked together about our troubles. Even though he would not let me have any contact with my mother, my mother's family, or the Roseberry family whom I loved so much, I was thankful to be with my father. He was my lifeline, and I wanted to be a good boy and not cause him any trouble. It was during this time with my father that I began to internalize my Core Beliefs about security, affection, and control—*be good, perform to please, and be strong.*

I worked to appear strong even though I was scared to death on the inside. At nine and ten years old, I was still wetting the bed at night. I was a good athlete, socially skilled, and knew how to perform in ways that made others like me. At the age of twelve, I even started waiting tables and learning to cook at a short-order restaurant owned by one of my father's friends. I started learning how to deal with the public, and I felt good about making some money to take care of my needs. I was acting out of my Core Beliefs to be good, to perform to please, and to be strong—all based upon my Core Wound of being abandoned and the resultant Core Lie that I was alone and it was all up to me.

I was acting out of my Core Beliefs to be good, to perform to please, and to be strong—all based upon my Core Wound of being abandoned and the resultant Core Lie that I was alone and it was all up to me.

What little peace I had began to disappear. In 1955, when I was twelve years old, my father remarried. I had high hopes that my brothers, sister, and I could be reunited again and live together in our own house. I was expecting a new beginning, and I was excited. My hopes once again were dashed. My dad's new wife was twenty-five years old and very insecure. She was jealous of any attention that my father gave to his children, and she was prone to fits of rage and depression. My new stepmom worked hard for our family, but she played the role of a martyr. The way I perceived her was untrusting, hardworking, mean, and unforgiving. The atmosphere in our home was tense, hostile, and emotionally unsafe. Whereas my birth mother was an alcoholic, my stepmother was a rageoholic. There was door slamming, arguing, and blaming. I stayed on the outs with her most of the time. I stayed away from home as much as I could. My dad was too passive to be of much help. One time when my stepmother demanded that I be given a spanking, my dad took me into the bathroom and hit the commode with his belt while asking me to yell so that my stepmother would think he was giving me a good beating. This situation just reinforced my Core Lie of being alone and made me depend even more on my Core Belief that I must remain strong.

My personal struggles remained hidden throughout my teen years. I didn't act out because I didn't want to run the risk of rejection. I looked good on the outside, but I was dying on the inside. I felt my life was in a lot of unconnected pieces. I was experiencing sexual awakenings that had no place to go, and I did not have a place or the language to express the physical and emotional feelings that were welling up inside me. I was left with feelings of shame and guilt for the desires of my heart. No one had prepared me for what I was experiencing. Again, my home situation created another blow to my Core Wound of abandonment and reinforced my Core Lie that I was alone. This made me stay close to my Core Beliefs of being good, performing to please, staying strong, and showing no weakness.

I began to make some important decisions that would set a course for the rest of my life.

I can't say I was very religious as a teen. I went to church on Sunday and found people of faith who cared for me. These caring people caused me to feel that God knew me and was concerned about me. I think I had a healthy concept of God for a kid, and I knew for certain that He had a special love for children. This meant a lot to me. One Sunday I really seemed to hear what the preacher was saying about God's love for me and how I should respond to that love. I was baptized.

My dad's response minimized what had just happened to me when he said, "Well, we had another dunking today!"

There were no big changes that others could see as a result of what I had done, but something happened inside me that day that caused me to realize that God was real and that He loved me. In spite of my Core Wound, my Core Lie, and my survival-oriented Core Beliefs, the Core Truths that I am loved and not alone began to break into my life view.

The remainder of my teen years and the time I spent in college were not without times of brokenness, despair, and making bad choices. I remember thinking after I got drunk during my freshman year at Ole Miss, *My mother was an alcoholic, my grandfather was an alcoholic, and I guess I am an alcoholic.* I knew I didn't want to give my children what my parents gave me. I wanted more out of life.

I felt drawn even closer to my faith and a belief in something greater than myself. Yet even in this effort I was frustrated. A minister who was my good friend and who I had learned to trust went through a divorce. Again, I felt despair as I thought, *If the minister can't make it, how in the world can someone as messed up as me make it in life?* I left the University of Mississippi for Harding University. I realized I was going to have to take responsibility for my own life and that I could not place anyone else on such a pedestal that they could tell me how to live.

> I realized I was going to have to take responsibility for my own life.

As I finished college and began my career as a teacher and counselor, I came to realize that I could not depend upon family, friends, or even church for direction in my life. I knew that my life needed to be guided by unchanging and foundational truths. Even though I knew this, I had difficulty overcoming something within me that kept establishing an inner authority that made me think and act in ways that were contrary to what I intended. My response was to be remorseful, pray harder, and try harder, but I kept on making the same mistakes. It was only after I systematically began to revisit the story of my family of origin, and got serious about the Core Story process, that I began to gain the insights that I have just shared—the insights necessary for me to discover and interpret the Core Wound, the Core Lie, and the faulty Core Beliefs that held such influence over me.

By following a deliberate, systematic approach to examining what I was thinking and why, I came to realize that I had a relational treasure in my wife, Charlotte, and my four daughters. I saw that I was not abandoned anymore and that I was not alone in my struggles. I exposed the Core Lies that I was responsible for how others felt, that I was obligated to please others, and that I could not be vulnerable. I replaced my Core Lies with the Core Truths that I have immeasurable value and that I am forgiven and loved—as a friend, a husband, a father, and as a Christian believer.

The Core Story process in which I engaged helped me to understand that I was holding on to Core Beliefs that were no longer true, necessary, or useful. They were beliefs that were causing me personal pain and relational problems. I saw that it was reasonable and safe to let my emotional child grow up and become an adult. I came to see the need to unhitch the wagon loaded with immature, trauma-induced, and flawed Core Beliefs from the bicycle of my life. I was being slowed down, and I was pedaling much too hard.

Have my Core Wounds, Core Lies, and faulty Core Beliefs been erased? Do I bask every day in the enlightenment of my Core Truths? Absolutely not! What I gained through the Core Story process was awareness and understanding, not amnesia. I must remind myself every day of my Core Truths, recommit to being truly present in the moment with my relationships, especially with my wife, and resist any tendency to backslide into toxic ways of thinking.

I want my life to personify the famous quote from the *I Have a Dream* speech given by Dr. Martin Luther King, Jr. on the steps of the Lincoln Memorial in Washington, D.C., on August 28, 1963:

"Free at last, free at last, thank God almighty I'm free at last."

CHAPTER 7

Unity

Unity is one of the best measures to indicate the quality of a relationship. Without unity being married is little more than two people doing their own thing while living together. Without unity there is an absence of the synergy that results when two people pull together in the same direction in such a way that the load of fulfilling relational commitments and responsibilities is equally shared.

The goal of unity is generally understood intellectually, but the achievement of unity comes about through the integrating activity of the spiritual dimension of personality. Unexamined and if not impacted by spiritual considerations, Core Beliefs tend to lean toward the side of self-interest. Self-interest is an antagonist to unity. Below is a diagram of our concept of a Unity Pyramid.

UNITY

RESPECT

UNDERSTANDING

COMMUNICATION

VALUES

CORE BELIEFS

Our conviction is that unity in being married is possible as a result of the mutual respect that develops as understanding is gained through meaningful communication. This communication reflects the values that each spouse holds as influenced by foundational Core Beliefs.

Exploring Core Beliefs is where you must start if your goal is to experience marital unity. You and your spouse need to define what you think it takes to keep you intact by answering questions such as *What am I not willing to change? What am I willing to share?* and *What am I willing to give up?* An awareness of Core Beliefs is so important because beliefs about safety and security, power and control, and affection and esteem influence every attempt to achieve unity. These beliefs are the basis for your ideas about how to present yourself, what to expect from others, and how to remain emotionally intact. Your Core Beliefs will either help you along or put up a roadblock to establishing the shared values, level of communication, depth of understanding, and respect for one another that will be necessary if unity is your goal.

Core Beliefs will act as a lens that determines how you view the four "C's" of unity—compromise, concession, cooperation, commitment. Your self-perception—how you see yourself and your needs—will greatly influence how you see others and their needs, especially your spouse. Your self-perception—what you think is necessary to define and defend yourself, a product of your Core Beliefs—can, without your awareness, sabotage your efforts to experience unity by asserting your needs over the needs of your marital relationship. It is crucial that deep-seated, self-protective Core Beliefs, Core Wounds, and Core Lies be identified, and if necessary confronted, if unity is to be achieved with your spouse. Faulty or dysfunctional Core Beliefs will interfere with movement toward the top of the unity pyramid.

Unity comes about when there is an alignment of effort and emphasis, when a couple is not living their lives at cross purposes. Unity will not come about just because it is a goal. Unity emerges when a couple's lives are complementary to one another. Unity comes about when a couple is moving together in the same direction following a path determined by the same values. The motive for seeking unity must be more than an attempt to please or avoid an argument. If unity becomes little more than a perpetual compromise, it will become tiresome if not arising out of shared goals and values.

If unity becomes little more than a perpetual compromise, it will become tiresome if not arising out of shared goals and values.

One way of describing unity is to make a comparison with musical harmony. Musically, harmony is created when differing notes are in accord with one another, thus becoming complementary sounds. The result of musical harmony is a sound that is fuller, richer, and more pleasing to the ear. It takes harmony achieved consistently over time, over many measures, to create a song. So it is when purpose, effort, and recognition are in harmony over time that the song of marital unity is played.

But unity in being married is not sameness. Unity does not require a couple becoming clones of one another. Such things as interests, friends, temperament, aptitude, background, and ethnicity don't have to be the same for unity to exist. Sharing things in common helps to promote unity but doesn't ensure unity. But there are three values that a couple must share if there is to be any hope for the development of relational unity. These shared values are always seeking to understand, making time for substantive communication, and showing respect for your spouse by always acting in their best interest.

Always seek to understand. Understanding a spouse requires insight, and insight comes from knowing. To know someone is to share in their struggles. Without truly caring about the one to whom you are married, you will not be willing to expend the time and effort, or exhibit the patience necessary to really get to know them and to walk intimately with them in both the good times and the bad. There is great wisdom expressed in this quote that is unclear as to its origin but unmistakable as to its meaning: "Seek first to understand and then to be understood."

Caring is not an endless stream of giving deference, making excuses, and extending forgiveness. Caring is wanting what is best for another, but deciding what is best takes knowledge and understanding. This insight can come through meaningful communication and the Core Story process because the information gained through these efforts is the first step in creating the progressive chain of knowing, then insight, then understanding.

Make time for substantive communication. Understanding is enhanced by listening to your spouse's point of view. Points of view are established during communication that has substance, is given time, is protected by respect for what is shared, is honest, and is transparent. And hearing is not listening. Listening is being undistracted, attentive, and genuinely interested in what is being shared. Listening is not responding prematurely to what is being shared.

Effective communication acknowledges each person's right to their own point of view without insisting on agreement. Many times, the best information to be gained from a conversation comes out of the most difficult portion of the exchange. Disagreement is less damaging to being married than a lack of understanding.

> Disagreement is less damaging to being married than a lack of understanding.

If the atmosphere in which conversation takes place is not safe, then meaningful and revelatory communication will not take place. Sharing personal thoughts requires vulnerability, and being vulnerable feels like being defenseless. If the vulnerability required for sharing is exploited in some way during conversation, this violation of sacred personal space will make further sharing unsafe and thus nonexistent. Without substantive communication involving both feelings and facts, there is no raw material with which to produce unity.

A tool that might be helpful in enhancing the quality and impact of conversations between a couple can be found in a workbook titled *Talking and Listening Together: Couple Communication 1* (1991) produced by Interpersonal Communication Programs, Inc. located in Littleton, Colorado. In this workbook authors Miller, Miller, Nunnally, and Wackman present a communication model termed the Awareness Wheel. In this model the authors stress that factors pertaining to sensations, actions, thoughts, intentions, and feelings must be identified and processed during the course of any meaningful attempt at communication between a husband and wife, especially when talking about difficult or emotionally charged topics.

Show respect for your spouse by attempting to act in their best interest. A key value that must be shared for unity to emerge is for you and your spouse to value your relationship so much that you both try to act in the best interest of one another. This component of respect between a married couple identifies and promotes the welfare of the other. It doesn't exploit or ridicule a weakness; it doesn't take advantage of a mistake; it doesn't withhold a favor; it doesn't employ relational competition where there are winners and losers. Mutual respect is an absolute prerequisite for unity to evolve.

The only way that the best interest of your spouse can be appreciated and for respect to be established is through understanding, and the path to understanding is through communication. You can't depend upon what you think you know about your spouse because what you think is determined by what you believe to be true, not what you learn from your spouse. Presumption is nothing more than a lazy analysis. It takes little effort to presume, and it is dangerous to do this because it represents only one point of view. The best interest of your spouse is best determined by careful

> *The only way that the best interest of your spouse can be appreciated and for respect to be established is through understanding, and the path to understanding is through communication.*

listening and keen, objective observation. Respect demands acting appropriately with due deference in every situation, and this attitude will go a long way toward promoting unity. A good resource for you to read is an out-of-print book by Paul Tournier titled *To Understand Each Other* (1966). This book is available over the internet through used book dealers.

Here is the testimony of one of the authors, Terry, that will illustrate how what has just been discussed has been put into place in his household.

A TESTIMONY FROM TERRY: UNIFYING ATTITUDES

My wife and I have sought to embrace these eight attitudes in our attempt to be unified in how we approach our relationship:

1. When you are wrong, admit it.
2. Do not hesitate to say, "I'm sorry" and mean it.
3. Commit this to one another, "I want what is best for you."
4. Commit this to one another, "Let's try to do the right thing."
5. Do not hesitate to declare, "I forgive you" and mean it.
6. Commit this to one another, "I will keep my word."
7. When offended, no matter the degree, make the first move toward reconciliation.
8. Commit this to one another, "I will make allowances for your bad day."

We have found that it is best to identify your own failure before pointing out the failure of your spouse. We try to meet one another in our humanity. We try to keep in mind the contamination of our Core Beliefs by our Core Lies which will, if we are not vigilant, invariably pull both of us in the direction of self-condemnation or unrealistic expectations. We have both benefitted from reading a book by Jim Woodroof titled *Sayings That Saved My Sanity: Journey to Freedom.*

Living the attitudes mentioned in Jim's book provided us with "invisible power" on a daily basis.

●   ●   ●   ●   ●

What then is the source of the psychic energy that can move a married couple upward through the various layers of the unity pyramid and toward the goal of unity? The source of this energy is determination. It is the shared commitment to put into action what needs to be done. It is being "all in." It is devotion to a course of action and a shared belief that the action chosen will be productive and successful.

But what is involved when making a commitment? Making a commitment begins with learning all that is involved. The cost of making a commitment must first be counted and proper preparation made. Carrying out a commitment will take time, energy, sacrifice, endurance, and the will to work until the goal is attained.

Making a commitment begins by seeking answers to important questions. *Will any training or additional study be required? Will what is expected from me be more than I am prepared to deliver? Am I willing to set aside the time and make any other sacrifices that will be necessary to fulfill what I have committed to do? Will I be willing to be challenged or to change if required to fulfill my commitment?*

Fulfilling a commitment means keeping it in the front of your mind and making it a part of your routine. Commitments require specific communication with your spouse so as to be able to properly coordinate and make any necessary adjustments. The means of measurement need to be established so that there is a standard by which to monitor progress in fulfilling commitments.

Carrying through on a mutually agreed upon commitment to work toward unity requires some structure where the execution of the commitment is orderly and predictable. Mutually agreed upon ground rules can help. These are the guidelines for conducting relational transactions on a daily basis. Negotiated ground rules make living together more equitable, workable, and predictable.

Consider this approach that Ron and his wife put in place early in their relationship in the pursuit of unity.

🔗 A TESTIMONY FROM RON: OUR RELATIONAL GROUND RULES

1. We will both seek out and honor biblically-based truth for guidance in our personal lives and in being married.
2. If there is to be a disagreement, arguments will relate to the present and not to the past.
3. Personal attacks are off-limits.
4. No personal criticism is to be expressed in the presence of a third party.
5. Parents and relatives will not to be brought into disagreements—we will forget and they will not.
6. We will not over extend ourselves so as to become dependent upon a second income to meet our expenses.
7. All household money will be shared money; there will be no separate household bank accounts.
8. All significant expenditures will be discussed in advance.
9. Housekeeping chores will be shared.
10. Ten percent of our bring-home pay will be contributed for the benefit of others.
11. There may be disagreements but no arguments in front of the children.
12. We will develop a shared philosophy of how best to discipline our children.

The development of these ground rules was very deliberate. Except for agreements about the children, the other ground rules were set in place soon after the wedding.

• • • • •

Love must be the main nutrient of being married. With this point in mind, one of the best definitions of the qualities of love that will promote and support marital unity is found in the New Testament in 1 Corinthians 13.

Love is patient, love is kind. It does not envy, it does not boast, it is not proud. It does not dishonor others, it is not self-seeking, it is not easily angered, it keeps no record of wrongs. Love does not delight in evil but rejoices with the truth. It always protects, always trusts, always hopes, always perseveres. Love never fails.

Experiencing unity is not easy. Two people living in relational harmony requires an intentional and sustained effort. Couples need to be heard and understood. It will take love like that just described to subdue self-interest and submit to the common interest that is so necessary if unity in being married is to ever be enjoyed.

CHAPTER 8

What It Will Take to Move Forward

If you are uncomfortable or dissatisfied in being married, you undoubtedly want to be heard. The first person listening to you needs to be you. What needs to be heard is not what someone else says about you but what you hear from exploring your own personal story. The problem is that listening to yourself is a hard thing to do. We are trying to assist you by making this effort less daunting.

If you did not desire an intimate, meaningful, fulfilling relationship with someone, you never would have married. This is why there is frustration and disappointment when the relationship does not turn out the way you intended or imagined. You ask yourself, *What happened? Why have things been complicated by conflicts and disillusionment? What can be done to improve my relationship?*

To begin to answer these questions you must first take a good look at yourself. Too often blame creates a cover for not examining your own contribution to marital problems. Making improvements in being married starts with you better understanding "the what" and "the how" of your contributions to the relationship.

Here is a real-life example of how serious self-contemplation can be beneficial in moving forward in the pursuit of a more fulfilling way to live.

> *Making improvements in being married starts with you better understanding "the what" and "the how" of your contributions to the relationship.*

A STORY FROM TERRY: WHAT DO I REALLY WANT?

After sixteen years of being married, I was burned out and confused. I was not clear in my thinking and our relationship was not meeting my expectations. I was at an emotional low and depressed. At the age of forty-one, I took a sabbatical from work and spent some serious time in contemplation. I focused on the question, *What do I really want?* I knew that my dark side was perfectly capable of answering this question by making it all about me. I knew I had to take the risk of self-inquiry because it could help the relationship between my wife and me.

Out of this time of decompression and meditation I decided what I really wanted more than anything else. I identified four principles that would guide me:

1. I want to think clearly.
2. I want to walk securely.
3. I want to live boldly.
4. I want to love faithfully.

We live life forward, but we understand it backward. Looking at where I was, where I had come from, and where I wanted to go helped me develop the focus I needed to live a life that was intentional, undistracted, and consistent.

• • • • •

It is understood that some difficulties in being married are obvious, serious, and may require separation or divorce to solve. Psychological, verbal, and physical abuse cannot be tolerated. Neglect and disinterest are more subtle but no less destructive to the relationship between a husband and wife. But other less obvious factors can also erode being married, such as chronic interactive deficits. These deficits are often unknown and unintended and can only be identified through a deliberate, structured investigative process such as the Core Story approach detailed in Section 2.

Relationally destructive Core Beliefs can be at the root of your problems. You may be working very hard at being a better marital partner, but working smarter at improving your relationship will be more effective than just working harder. What you perceive is happening between you and your spouse and what in reality is taking place will be determined principally by the psychological lens through which you are looking. As was pointed out in Chapter 4, the components of this psychological lens are your Core Beliefs, and these beliefs will either create a focused or a blurred view of what is actually going on.

This is where the Core Story process comes into play. The Core Story process is a valuable tool for hearing your own story and identifying the factors that make you see yourself, others, and the world as you do. The exploration of your Core Story is what it will take for you to move forward with any renewed insight.

The Core Story process is where the combination of a visual, cognitive, and experiential approach to personal story discovery will permit you to see and hear your own life experiences in the context of how they came about. . This Core Story process will not fix your problems, but this approach can provide you with the insight you will need to better understand the rules you have adopted for how you will conduct yourself, perceive others, and interpret the give and take involved in being married.

Through the Core Story process, you will see and hear through your own account using your own language how your Core Beliefs developed about staying safe, being in control, and maintaining self-esteem. These are critical elements in the construction of your self-perception. You will discover why these Core Beliefs are so important to you and why they have maintained a controlling influence in your life since childhood. When you hear yourself and recount the formation of your story, you will have a clearer vision of why you think the way you do and why your self-image, your view of others, and your worldview may be contributing to tensions within the relationship with your spouse, discomfort within yourself, or both.

There is an important point that needs to be made as we examine the transformational potential of knowing your Core Story. Even after identifying your Core Beliefs, even after discovering any Core Lies, don't assume enlightenment alone will motivate you to take the actions necessary for self-improvement. Fear and denial are proven de-motivators for change—even constructive change.

Knowing your personal story and making a commitment to address Core Wounds and any dysfunctional Core Beliefs are two different things. Take this story, a personal account by Ron, to illustrate this point.

A STORY FROM RON: KNOWING BUT DENYING

I emotionally broadsided my wife in the first year of being married when one of my Core Wounds, one of which I was well aware, rendered me incapable of completing the medical education I had hoped for, planned for, and worked for since I was in the sixth grade. In May 1970, she married a medical student at the half-way point of his first year. In March of 1971, she found herself married to an ER tech who had dropped out of school. On the surface this appeared as a cruel relational bait and switch.

A Core Wound was created for me when I was fifteen years old as a result of a frightful and embarrassing emotional collapse after I witnessed a bus accident involving my peers. The front bus in a two-bus caravan returning from a summer youth event left the slick pavement, went up an embankment, and turned onto its side. There were kids, luggage, blood, and broken glass everywhere. I entered the bus to help remove crash victims through an emergency door on the roof and helped attend to the victims till first responders arrived.

All of the uninjured were taken to the closest bus terminal to await another bus. It was there that I had an anxiety attack and had to be medicated in order to ride the bus home. I embarrassed myself and felt like a failure at what I had tried to do in helping others.

This entire experience so troubled me that I developed what today is termed post-traumatic stress disorder (PTSD). Anytime something occurred that reminded me of this bus accident and my failure to hold up in this situation resulted in a panic attack. Throughout high school and college, I pushed through the anxiety created by films shown at the Future Physicians Club, specimen dissections in biology classes, and dressing wounds as the first aid provider at summer camp. I was ashamed of my feelings and basically denied the implication of these feelings on my goal of becoming a physician. My wife and I were not seasoned enough in our relationship for me to unpack all of my doubts and fears to her. I rationalized that I could just continue to tough it out and push through my panic attacks as I had done in the past, but I was self-delusional and wrong.

I was aware of my significant dysfunction when I married. I had put off any serious attempt to address my PTSD because of my fear of facing the fear. My problem was I did not have the courage to act on what I knew needed to be done. My Core Beliefs, the guardian of my self-perception, tasked me to avoid confronting my Core Lie, thus avoiding the perceived damage to my self-esteem by walking away from the accolades of being a medical student.

Once I came clean with my wife about my real feelings, she proved by her tough love and support that she had married me, not a medical student. By opening up to others and dealing honestly with myself, I realized I had waited too long to salvage my medical studies and would have to take another career path. With the help of a wife who believed in me more than I believed in myself, I repurposed my interest and aptitude to become a hospital administrator. By the fifth year of being married and my graduation from the Medical College of Virginia with a degree in hospital administration, her story and my story became our story. Acting together to deal with my hidden truth brought us closer together as a couple.

* * * * *

Revisiting and clarifying your personal story is only the first step toward what it takes to move forward in being better at being married. The purpose of this book is not just to provide definitions and descriptions but to have you own what you learn about yourself and to have you use what you learn to improve yourself and your relationships, especially with your spouse. Movement toward improvement is the goal.

For the most part you already know factually what it takes to be successfully married. It's learning and admitting how you actually are that takes the hard work. The Core Story is a tool in this process of discovery and improvement. Once you have outed your cluster of controlling Core Beliefs, you can source the people and the information that can help you better understand what you have learned and help you develop a plan for next steps.

It will be helpful if you are open and transparent with your spouse about trying to overcome any adverse influence your Core Wounds, Core Lies, and faulty Core Beliefs are having on your relationship. Ideally you and your spouse will be able to work together on some areas of mutual self-improvement, but this is not necessary for you to address your own issues and make progress on your own.

Your commitment to work on being better at being married should not be dependent on the support or involvement of your spouse. You bolster your own integrity by attempting to be your best self within the means provided by your knowledge and capabilities. Your spouse may become better able to relate to you as a direct result of you being able to better relate to them.

Moving through personal transformation is not easy, but the work involved is not physically hard. It is emotionally hard because it requires a candid admission that you may be flawed or incomplete in some way. To make such an admission requires humility, and humility takes mental work to subdue the tendency to be defensive when questioned or challenged.

Following through with the personal improvements that humility allows you to acknowledge requires a commitment. And a commitment requires allotting the time, energy, and effort necessary to actually implement desired change.

There's more. The pathway along which a commitment must move toward its fulfillment must be kept clear of obstacles. There are two main obstacles that you need to look out for.

The first of the two obstacles is fear. Fear will allege that there will be a horrible, debilitating, humiliating result if there is any attempt at self-discovery or personal transformation. Fear develops when there is a perceived threat, and where there is fear there will be the attempt to create a protective defense.

Conducting a critical examination of the Core Beliefs that you have depended upon since childhood to support and defend your well-being can be intimidating and unsettling. Your natural tendency will be avoidance or rationalizing that the problem is not really as bad as it appears. The mere hint that important Core Beliefs aren't working in your favor and may need to change is scary in and of itself!

> *Conducting a critical examination of the Core Beliefs that you have depended upon since childhood to support and defend your well-being can be intimidating and unsettling.*

Fortunately, there are some antidotes with which to treat the poison of fear. Searching out good information is one antidote. Learning what others who are qualified and have been vetted have to say about the issues of Core Belief can help remove some of the unknowns that feed fear. Finding out that others have experienced the same relational issues you are facing and have benefited from critical, structured self-inquiry will give you confidence to keep moving toward your goal of personal transformation. The psychiatrist Karl Menninger said, "Fears are educated into us, and can, if we wish, be educated out."

The other antidote for the poison of fear is courage. To be clear, courage allows you to work around fear but does not remove fear. Civil rights activist Rosa Parks, who in 1955 would not move to the back of her bus in Montgomery, Alabama, is known to have said this: "Knowing what must be done does away with fear." She is talking about the power of conviction which is the substance of commitment. Conviction takes you beyond just knowing and powers you through the apprehension that could derail you from doing what needs to be done.

Fear also can have a constructive role where change is involved. Personal change should not be impulsive. Not everyone's life is a train wreck, and sometimes as a result of the Core Story process a person finds there is very little about the way they think that needs to change. Rather than be an obstacle to personal transformation, fear can be the companion of caution where commitments are first studied, planned, and wisely implemented. The voice of fear should be heard but not allowed to become your spokesperson.

Now we want you to consider the second of the two main obstacles in the pathway along which a commitment must move. This is pride. Pride removes even the possibility that Core Beliefs may be contributing to you being incomplete, wrong, ineffective, or unlikeable in any way. Pride will dominate a relationship by obsessing on who is right, not what is right.

Pride will dominate a relationship by obsessing on who is right, not what is right.

The admission that you need to make changes in some of the ways you think and act, along with the realization that you may have caused relational damage is likely to cause you to feel shame and remorse. To move further along the pathway of your commitment to being better at being married, you will need to be able to forgive yourself. Forgiveness will permit you to look forward with optimism, not backward with paralyzing shame, as you embrace Core Truths.

There is still one more step to be taken once fear and pride have been subdued, the Core Story process completed, and a sincere commitment made to correct or improve your marital relationship. You must seek out information that can be accepted at an intellectual, emotional, and spiritual level as superior to what you already think to be true. This substitution of "my" information with "their" information is an act of faith.

Faith is functionally your willingness to accept and act upon as truth something that you did not experience or develop yourself. Information that is validated as reliable because it has been sustainable and renewable over time is information that can be trusted. Trusted information becomes a belief, and belief that accepts the risks and anticipates the benefits of expression becomes an act of faith.

Caution, not fear, is warranted when choosing new sources of information around which to remodel your Core Beliefs. New bad information is of no more use to you than your old bad information. We have a recommendation for you to consider.

A relevant, reliable, time tested, readily accessible, and understandable source of information about how best to live your life and be married is the Bible. Much of what you are searching for as a means to better interpret your Core Story and make appropriate changes in your ways of thinking and acting can be found in the Bible. Faith in what is written in the Bible does not require church membership or any particular religious affiliation. To mankind in general the Bible can serve as a guide for better living and building relationships.

If you can overlook the use of the Bible by some religious organizations as the basis for forced dogma, coercion, and institutional perpetuation, you will be able to consider the Bible as a trustworthy source of information about how you can best live your life, be in community with others, and be your best at being married.

If you can figure out how to be the best you, you can live free of self-imposed despair and will experience more joy in your relationships.

SECTION 2

The Core Story Process

What a person believes will override what they know. Controlling beliefs often lie beyond conscious awareness and must be sought out. – Terry S. Smith

A video of a Core Story interview can be viewed by going to
www.coachinglifematters.com
and selecting Videos. There you will find the Core Story Training Video.

CHAPTER 9

The Approach to the Core Story Process

You are now ready to begin the Core Story process. It is possible to complete the process alone, but it is preferable if you involve your spouse, a friend, or a member of your family to help. Involving your spouse as your partner in the exercise will not only give them a deeper insight into the elements that make up your personality; their involvement will also stimulate discussion and feedback that will result in deeper understanding that will in turn enrich being married.

Organizing your thoughts to respond to the questions in the following chapter may cause you to consider things you have never considered before, or at least not in a long time. The structure of the process may reveal information to your spouse that is important to their understanding of you and be information they have never heard before.

> *The structure of the process may reveal information to your spouse that is important to their understanding of you and be information they have never heard before.*

Even if your Core Story process is part of a session with a minister, counselor, or life coach, you will benefit. If your spouse is present with you, he or she will benefit from your storytelling in this setting as well.

When referring to the Core Story, we are referring to the process of mapping your relational history over the first eighteen years of life (with a particular emphasis on your early childhood beliefs about security, esteem, and power). During the process, you (or the person you are helping) will recount a relational history covering three generations. Also to be recounted will be the experiences and perceptions of a wide range of relationships, including how you feel you were perceived by your parents.

Keep in mind that the completion of the Core Story process will not always result in the discovery of some hidden flaw. Some people will complete this process in order to see if there are things about them that, if known, might make being married even better. Sometimes the Core Story effort will only result in a confirmation that there is little about your actions and personality that are detrimental to being married.

COMPLETING THE CORE STORY PROCESS ALONE OR IN PARTNERSHIP WITH A SPOUSE OR FRIEND.

Before jumping to the Core Story questions, carefully read Chapter 10 to see all that will be involved and learn more about what is to be accomplished. You need to become familiar with the various questions, forms, and formats you will encounter. The Core Story process builds upon itself as you go through the steps, so following the process in the sequence prescribed is necessary for you to properly build upon your personal story and get the most out of your storytelling experience.

Both you and your spouse going through the Core Story regimen together, usually on two different occasions, can be very useful in developing the mutual understanding that is so important to being married. Taking this approach allows each of you to facilitate the other through the various stages of the exercise. You can then hear one other's story while benefitting from a second perspective on what is being shared and interpreted.

COMPLETING THE CORE STORY PROCESS IN A PROFESSIONAL SETTING.

You may encounter the Core Story process as part of a help session with a trained professional. Your minister, counselor, or life coach will have chosen this interview tool to assist in gathering the information that they need to better help you and to provide a tool that will help you gain valuable insight about yourself.

The Core Story process as refined by Terry Smith is conceptually and educationally sound. That is why this tool was chosen. It employs the widely used think-pair-share learning strategy. It supports multi-sensory learning techniques where what is heard and what is recorded on the Core Story diagram become companion learning tools.

The Core Story process is also consistent with Visual Learning Strategies (VLS). This is where images are used to help a person reflect on their own thinking. This approach facilitates learning through reasoning with evidence, making connections, wondering and asking questions, uncovering complexity and going below the surface of things, identifying patterns and making generalizations, and evaluating evidence, arguments, and actions.

By employing the Visual Learning Strategies inherent to the Core Story process, critical thinking is enhanced through a discussion about the visual representation captured on the Core Story diagram. This learning method has proven to be a good way for tapping into a person's background knowledge and aiding in memory recall.

Many people have experienced some degree of hurt and trauma as a child. Misinformation has been internalized as truth. Unfortunately, children vividly record what happens to them, but are ill-equipped to properly interpret what has happened. A child's unconscious solutions to grappling with misfortune and misinformation often prove counterproductive once reaching adulthood.

> *Unfortunately, children vividly record what happens to them, but are ill-equipped to properly interpret what has happened.*

Move now to the next chapter and engage in the Core Story process.

CHAPTER 10

The Steps in the Core Story Process

A. Tools

Prepare to visually capture the results of the Core Story process. A whiteboard, chalkboard, flipchart, or just a piece of paper can be used to diagrammatically depict the answers to the series of questions detailed throughout this chapter. Use the templates and charts below only as suggestions as to how you might map out a Core Story. Feel free to customize any of the templates or charts to fit your particular story. Some Core Stories will be more complex than others and some stories will have more family members and conflicts than others. Some Core Story maps can end up very congested with information. But the purpose of the Core Story Template is to capture the story, not to complete a neat chart.

You will find it useful to have writing instruments of different colors to use in recording different categories of response. For example, you might use the color black to record names, green to depict any troubling relationships, red for the stars in the story, and blue for the list of Core Wounds, Core Lies, and Core Truths.

The first illustration below is a template to use in organizing the story board. This template is to be used to capture the answers to the questions in Part B of this chapter. The second illustration is related to the first in that it is a chart illustrating various symbols that can be used to denote the responses to the questions in Part C of this chapter.

The third illustration below is to be used to capture the responses to the questions appearing in Parts F and G of this chapter. The fourth illustration below is to serve as a prompter to help with the answers to the questions in Parts F and G. There is no right answer to these questions, and the list of possible answers is not intended to be all inclusive. The most appropriate answer to a question may not even appear on the list in the illustration. The best answer is the answer given by the one being interviewed.

The fifth and sixth illustrations below are to show what a completed Core Story map might look like. This example is very neat for the purposes of illustration, but don't expect the one you construct as you conduct the Core Story exercise to be so neat. No matter how busy or complicated a Core Story map becomes, it will be a meaningful representation to the one being interviewed of the generational layers of relationships that have helped to create the system of beliefs that are being identified.

CORE STORY FRAMEWORK
Sample

PATERNAL

Grandfather

_____
_____
_____

Grandmother

_____
_____
_____

MATERNAL

Grandfather

_____
_____
_____

Grandmother

_____
_____
_____

Grandfather   Grandmother

Brother   Sister

Grandfather   Grandmother

Brother Brother Sister (Adopted)

Father

Brother   Sister

Mother

FATHER

_____
_____
_____

YOU

MOTHER

_____
_____
_____

SCHOOL

6-12   12-15   16-18

_____   _____   _____
_____   _____   _____
_____   _____   _____

RELIGIOUS COMMUNITY
Islam, Hinduism, Buddhism, Jewish: (Orthodox, Reformed, Conservative), Christian

12-15   16-18

_____   _____
_____   _____
_____   _____

CORE STORY
Symbol Chart

—#— DIVORCE	—/— SEPARATION
WWW CONFLICT	• • • • • DISTANCE
～～～ AFFAIR	✕✕✕✕✕ ABUSE
┊ ADOPTION	══ CLOSENESS
☐ MALE	◯ FEMALE
TRAGEDY	DEATH
CUT OFF	AWARENESS OF THOSE WHO LOVED & AFFIRMED YOU

CORE STORY FRAMEWORK
Sample

PROCESS OUTCOME	OBJECTIVE
CORE BELIEFS	**DISCOVER**
Safety and Security	
Affection and Esteem	
Power and Control	
CORE WOUND	**EXPOSE**
CORE LIE	**RENOUNCE**
CORE TRUTH	**REPLACE**

CORE STORY
Examples of Core Beliefs

SECURITY/SURVIVAL

- Be good
- Obey
- Be perfect
- Work hard
- Be invisible
- Be silent
- Other

CORE WOUND

- Abandoned
- Rejected
- Outcast
- Invisible/Not seen
- Other

AFFECTION/ESTEEM

- Perform to please
- Achieve to please
- Be the best
- Be attractive
- Be helpful
- Other

CORE LIE

- I am worthless.
- I am not good enough.
- I am less than.
- I am a failure.
- Other

POWER/CONTROL

- Be funny/humorous
- Be nice/complicit
- Be cute
- Be strong/Show no weakness
- Be smart
- Other

CORE TRUTH

- I am of immeasurable value.
- I am loved.
- I am forgiven.
- I am a not alone.
- I am a gift.
- Other

PATERNAL

MATERNAL

Grandfather

Absent
Alcoholic
Non-Religious

Grandmother

Smart
Tough
Non-Religious

Grandfather

Kind
Absent
Religious/Christian

Grandmother

Independent
Artistic
Religious/Christian

Jack
79
Military

Mary
77
Teacher

Joe
80

Liz
83
Homemaker

Grandfather

Grandmother

Grandfather

Grandmother

52

Brother
57

Sister

61

45

35

Brother Brother Sister (Adopted)

Tense

Jim
60
Engineer

Jane
59
Homemaker

Fred
63
Banker

Father

Mother

Jerry
40

Liz
35

Brother

Bud
38

Sister

FATHER

YOU

MOTHER

Busy
Strict
Alcoholic
Non-religious

Kind/Available
Quiet
Religious/Christian

SCHOOL

RELIGIOUS COMMUNITY
Islam, Hinduism, Buddhism, Jewish: (Orthodox, Reformed, Conservative), Christian

6-12	12-15	16-18
Positive	Negative	Positive
Teachers	Bullied	Sports
Friends	Good Grades	Friends
		Good Grades

12-15	16-18
Good Teachers	Too Strict
Camp	Unwelcome
Friends	Judged

CORE STORY FRAMEWORK
Sample

PROCESS OUTCOME	OBJECTIVE
CORE BELIEFS	DISCOVER

Safety and Security

Obey

Affection and Esteem

Be helpful

Power and Control

Be strong / show no weakness

CORE WOUND	EXPOSE

Rejected

CORE LIE	RENOUNCE

Not good enough

CORE TRUTH	REPLACE

I am forgiven

B. Family of Origin Questions

These questions are given in a sequence that will support an orderly unfolding of a person's Core Story. Working through these questions and visually recording the responses makes this a visual, cognitive, and experiential endeavor.

The answers to these simple questions can create strong emotions. It is important, should you be helping another person work through the Core Story process, to listen closely and be present in these moments. You should begin by stating this is a very personal and confidential meeting and you do not intend to share this story with anyone. Let it be known that you will give them a copy of their story when completed.

You will begin with questions about the father and the immediate nuclear family with whom you or the one being interviewed grew up during their first eighteen years. Use the Core Story Framework as well as the Symbols Chart just shown above to capture all the characters in the Core Story before asking the relational questions listed in Part C of this chapter. Sometimes the person you are assisting will be traumatized just by naming people in their family of origin. When this happens, let them know you will come back to these significant people in a moment.

It is all right if some of the questions are not answered as this lack of response can be revelatory in the storytelling process.

1. What is your father's name?
2. What did he do for a living when you were growing up?
3. How old is your father?
4. What is your mother's name?
5. Did your mother work outside of the home when you were growing up? If so, what did she do for a living?
6. How old is your mother?
7. How many brothers and sisters do you have? Where do you fit in? List the ages of the siblings from oldest to youngest. (This question is intended to put the storyteller on the Core Story diagram in the appropriate birth order as soon as possible.)

8. Did your parents stay married? If the answer is "no," who did they marry?

9. If your parents divorced, how old were you when this occurred?

10. How many brothers and sisters did your father have?

11. What are the ages of your father's siblings? Living or dead? Ages at death?

12. How many brothers and sisters does your mother have?

13. What are the ages of your mother's siblings? Living or dead? Ages at death?

14. What is the name of your father's father?

15. What is his age, if living? What was his age when he died?

16. What did your father's father do for a living?

17. What is the name of your father's mother?

18. What is her age, if living? What was her age when she died?

19. Did your father's mother work outside of the home? If so. what did she do for a living?

20. What is the name of your mother's father?

21. What is his age, if living? What was his age when he died?

22. What did your mother's father do for a living?

23. What is the name of your mother's mother?

24. What is her age, if living? What was her age when she died?

25. Did your mother's mother work outside of the home? If so, what did she do for a living?

C. Questions to Identify How Relationships Were Experienced

In asking these questions you will enter into your experiential world or that of the person being interviewed as it was understood to be. You will need the symbols for closeness, distance, conflict, and abuse listed under item A in the Symbols Chart at the beginning of this chapter. Use of these symbols will help create a visual, cognitive and experiential awareness of the story as it develops.

When helping another person work through the Core Story process, observe the body language very closely. Their mood or reactions to the questions may indicate the need to either move on or pursue additional questions. When asking these questions, allow the person time to answer. Do not be afraid of silence as it can produce some of the best responses.

1. How did you relate to your father growing up? Was he close or distant? Was he kind, mean, abusive, alcoholic, absent, religious, or non-religious? What spiritual tribe did your father subscribe to (e.g., Christian, Jewish, Muslim, Atheist, Buddhist, etc.)?

2. How did you relate to your mother growing up? Was she close or distant? Was she kind, mean, abusive, alcoholic, absent, religious, or non-religious? What spiritual tribe did your mother subscribe to (e.g., Christian, Jewish, Muslim, Atheist, Buddhist, etc.)?

3. If you have siblings, how did you experience them relating to your father (e.g., close, distant, combative, loving, etc.)?

4. How did you experience each of your siblings relating to your mother (e.g., close, distant, combative, loving, etc.)?

5. What was your relationship to each or your siblings growing up (e.g., close, distant, combative, loving, etc.)?

6. What was the atmosphere of your home (e.g., safe, loving, chaotic, hostile, unpredictable, welcoming, warm, combative, etc.)?

7. What are the descriptive adjectives your father would use to describe how he experienced his father when he was growing up? Was he close or distant? Was he kind, mean, abusive, alcoholic, absent, religious, or non-religious? What spiritual tribe did your father subscribe to (e.g., Christian, Jewish, Muslim, Atheist, Buddhist, etc.)?

8. What are the descriptive adjectives your father would use to describe how he experienced his mother growing up? Was she close or distant? Was she kind, mean, abusive, alcoholic, absent, religious, or non-religious? What spiritual tribe did his mother subscribe to (e.g., Christian, Jewish, Muslim, Atheist, Buddhist, etc.)?

9. What are the descriptive adjectives your mother would use to describe how she experienced her father when she was growing up? Was he close or distant? Was he kind, mean, abusive, alcoholic, absent, religious, or non-religious? What spiritual tribe did her father subscribe to (e.g., Christian, Jewish, Muslim, Atheist, Buddhist, etc.)?

10. What are the descriptive adjectives your mother would use to describe how she experienced her mother growing up? Was she close or distant? Was she kind, mean, abusive, alcoholic, absent, religious, or non-religious? What spiritual tribe did her mother subscribe to (e.g., Christian, Jewish, Muslim, Atheist, Buddhist, etc.)?

11. How did your father relate to each of his siblings (e.g., close, distant, combative, loving, etc.)?

12. How did your mother relate to each of her siblings (e.g., close, distant, combative, loving, etc.)?

13. 13. How did your father's father relate to each of your father's siblings (e.g., close, distant, combative, loving, etc.)?

14. 14. How did your father's mother relate to each of your father's siblings (e.g., close, distant, combative, loving, etc.)?

15. How did your mother's father relate to each of your mother's siblings (e.g., close, distant, combative, loving, etc.)?

16. How did your mother's mother relate to each of your mothers siblings (e.g., close, distant, combative, loving, etc.)?

17. How did your father's parents relate to you (e.g., close, distant, combative, loving, etc.)? How did they relate to your siblings?

18. How did your mother's parents relate to you (e.g., close, distant, combative, loving, etc.)? How did they relate to your siblings?

D. Questions to Identify Life Experiences Outside the Home

Many times significant experiences and influences occur for young and middle age children outside of their household. School, religious groups, sports participation, and adults other than their parents can make impressions that are formative and may last for a lifetime.

1. What was elementary, middle, and high school like for you? Were they a positive or negative experience? What were the reasons it was positive or negative for each? List those reasons. NOTE: The responses may be different for each different grade level.
2. What about your involvement in religious assemblies such as church, synagogue, or mosque? Was this involvement a positive or negative experience? List the reasons you feel as you do.
3. Were there any activities outside of school that were special to you growing up, such as a sports team, scouting, 4-H Club, playing in a band, etc.?
4. Were there adults other than any of your relatives who were very special to you growing up?

E. Questions to Identify Significant Caring People

It is now time to explore and reflect upon the special people growing up. This is the point in the Core Story process where you or the one being interviewed are to identify the people experienced as especially caring. These are the people who were always glad to see you.

1. Who were the people during your childhood who were special to you, who you experienced as valuing you, encouraging you, or who seemed delighted when you came into the room? Give each of these people a *big, red star* on the Core Story diagram.
2. Make a list of these significant caring people on a piece of paper. Take time to give thanks for each one of these people. It could be a mother, father, second grade teacher, neighbor, or best friend. It might be this special affirmation came from a pet or a character in a book or movie. If the names are not already on the Core Story diagram, add them somewhere.

F. Questions to Identify Controlling Beliefs

At this point in the Core Story process, reflect on all that has been shared so far, ponder what is displayed on the Core Story diagram, and decide what are believed to be the controlling beliefs that provided the most controlling influence while growing up.

In order to facilitate the identification of these Core Beliefs, answer the questions below. To assist in responding to these questions, refer to the Examples of Core Beliefs illustration in Part A, at the beginning of this chapter. This illustration presents only possible responses to be considered, and the most appropriate response to the questions may not appear on the list of examples.

1. Picturing yourself in your early teens, what did you think you needed to be safe? You may want to look at the Examples of Core Beliefs to prime your thinking for a possible response.
2. Picturing yourself in your early teens, what did you think you needed to gain affection and esteem? What did you decide that you needed to do to be loved? You may want to look at the Examples of Core Beliefs to prime your thinking for a possible response.
3. Picturing yourself in your early teens, what did you think you need to attain and hold power and control? What did you feel you needed to do in order to assert yourself? What did you decide that you needed to do in order to have control over how others perceived you? You may want to look at the Examples of Core Beliefs to prime your thinking for a possible response.
4. How do you prevent your thirteen year-old self from wrecking your life as an adult?

G. Questions to Identify the Core Wounds, Core Lies, and Core Truths

It is now time to apply the information gained through the Core Story process to identify how Core Beliefs may be reinforcing misconceptions about personal identity. A person's Core Beliefs are established early in life and represent how a person was able to navigate the world as a child. These early formed beliefs were counted on to provide a way to flourish or survive. Following these beliefs was a way to gain recognition and affirmation. These beliefs provided a way to gain some control of or power over individual circumstances.

However, the Core Beliefs that worked for the child may actually be toxic to the adult. These early-formed beliefs create a "false self" that may not serve an individual well when experiencing the stresses of adulthood. If you are helping another person work through the Core Story process, you might consider sharing some of your own experience with the "false self" in order to create a context for the next series of questions.

To facilitate this process of self-discovery, proceed as follows:

1. What might you consider to be your Core Wound? The Core Wound is a deep hurt, fear, or anger that results from childhood experience. Many people have a Core Wound by the time they are twelve years old. Even if an individual had what could be called a perfect loving home, the Core Wound many times surfaces when they imagine putting their arm around the 12-year-old self and asking the child within how they might have been wounded. Some people will say, "I have no wound." Allow them time to reflect. The wound may be deep and hard to recognize. Examples of some answers: abandoned, rejected, invisible, alone, etc. NOTE: If you are working with another person, never press them to give any more of the details of their Core Wound then they are willing to share comfortably.

2. What might you consider to be your Core Lie? The Core Lie centers on the deep feelings and perceptions a person has about him or herself, and these feelings will often persist into adulthood. The Core Lie is founded on misinterpretations, misconceptions, and reactions that a person has about their capabilities and potential. These misperceptions arise from their Core Wound. The Core Lie is at the end of a cascade of unconscious thought

that tries to make meaning of and adapt to a Core Wound that creates the basis for Core Beliefs that support Core Lies. Naming these Core Lies is a key step in an individual understanding what is fundamental in life and what is controlling their life. It is possible that up to 95 percent of a person's behavior is driven by their Core Lie. Examples could include: *I'm not good enough. I don't count. I'm less than. I'm responsible. It's my fault.*

3. Can you accept the premise of the existence of Core Truths? Core Truth is information that people must accept in faith believing that it is better than the information they have developed for themselves. A Core Truth, if it is accepted, will challenge but mitigate the faulty and dysfunctional Core Beliefs that have developed around Core Wounds and Core Lies.

H. Making the Decision

It is now time to realize that you get to decide how to respond to life. The awareness, mindfulness, and understanding that is represented in the following points will help you or the person you are helping get unstuck and begin moving toward hope and joy. Reflect on the personal empowerment expressed in these statements:

1. I get to *decide* to renounce and revoke my Core Lie.
2. I get to *choose* to replace my Core Lies with Core Truths.
3. I have the *ability* to change because I am larger than my pain, trauma, and circumstances. I will break free and not make friends with my pain.

Deciding to accept Core Truth is an internal spiritual matter for each person. Renouncing Core Lies on a daily basis is a spiritual process that will renew the mind and is supported through spiritual disciplines such as contemplation, meditation, listening, reading, journaling, etc. These constructive steps will help in healing, not forgetting.

The step to make life-changing decisions is often slow. Life is a marathon and not a sprint, as healing and personal transformation are lifelong processes.

I. Final Thoughts and Reflections

If you have been assisting another person work through the Core Story process, review and emphasize the following points:

1. Ask the person: What is the one thing you will take away from your own story today? Then, ask if they have any questions for you.
2. Ask the storyteller to look at the Core Story visual that has been created and share any interesting reflections or observations they might have.
3. If a friend, mate, or a small group is present, ask each person to share briefly how their story is similar or different. Then you, as the facilitator, can share with the person being interviewed how your story is similar or different. This need not be a long recitation but a brief connecting point of how your story may be connected to that of the person being interviewed.
4. Set up another meeting, with the only assignment being for the individual to reflect on their own story.

CHAPTER 11

Remarks on Healing Through Hearing and Understanding

As we conclude this section about the Core Story process, Terry Smith is the best one to write this chapter. Over his career he has continued to refine the genogram tool into what is now the Core Story. Terry provides first hand testimony about the universal usefulness of this process for personal story development, Core Belief identification, and the discovery of Core Truths.

● ● ● ● ●

What the Core Story process reveals is that our belief system is a composite of what we have learned and experienced on our own and what beliefs and impressions have been handed down generationally from our parents and relatives. The Core Story process is one way to discover that our system of personal beliefs may not be big enough or hardy enough to handle real life. The Core Story process is a tool to aid in looking for and reframing faulty beliefs.

We all have unmet emotional needs and expectations. We may look to being married, our work, or friends to meet these needs, and when these needs and expectations are not met we feel let down. We find that the personality traits we depended upon to get us through youth, the early-formed Core Beliefs, won't always serve us well as adults. When the beliefs

We find that the personality traits we depended upon to get us through youth, the early-formed Core Beliefs, won't always serve us well as adults.

we are depending upon begin to fail us, especially in being married, we will be judgmental of our own shortcomings and as equally judgmental of the shortcomings of others, even our spouse.

Physical and psychological trauma is a particularly tragic path for the formation of Core Beliefs. My experience has been that even the Core Wounds and Core Lies resulting from such trauma can be exposed, placed into a proper context, and thus lessened in their impact as a result of the Core Story process. I have worked my entire professional life with people throughout the United States who have experienced trauma. I have worked with combat veterans suffering from Post-Traumatic Stress Disorder (PTSD), male and female prison inmates, and children traumatized by parents who have abused their children physically, sexually, and mentally. I have also worked with people who have suffered emotional trauma due to failed relationships and harsh self-judgment.

I have also worked in India with victims of sex trafficking and alcoholics in rehabilitation clinics. In Nicaragua I worked with 12-year-old children who survived by carrying an AK-47 rifle. In Israel I met with the adult children of Holocaust survivors who had been beaten and abused by parents who survived the concentration camps but carried brutality and abuse into their homes. In El Salvador, Guyana, and Italy I worked with those who were also traumatized as children. In every case I found that the Core Story process helps people understand their story and provides a way for them to access and remodel their innermost world.

I was first introduced to the predecessor to the Core Story process, the genogram, in 1983 by a friend, Tim Lowry, who was a licensed Marriage and Family Therapist. This multi-generational diagram of family behavior patterns was developed in the 1940's by a psychiatrist, Murray Bowen and was documented in a book he co-authored with Michael Kerr titled *Family Evaluation*. Since then physicians and therapists have used the genogram tool to identify generational behavioral pathology.

As I developed and improved the Core Story process, the publications by several other behavioral professionals have helped me along the way. Dr. Merle R. Jordan, a professor at Boston University where I completed my doctorate degree, is the author of *Reclaiming your Story: Family History and Spiritual Growth*. I was also influenced a great deal by the thinking of Edwin Friedman, author of the book titled *Generation to Generation: Family Process in Church and Synagogue*, where he identifies and explains the power of the psychodynamic pressure that is present in familial relations. Thomas Keating's books titled *Invitation to Love* and *Open Mind-Open Heart* helped me to develop my concepts of Core Beliefs, Core Wounds, and Core Lies. The book titled *Refocusing Your Passions: A Christ-Centered Approach to Overcoming Addictive Behavior* by Don Crossland also proved to be useful.

The Core Story process has been a journey in the making and it is my hope that this tool provides a trustworthy method for helping people get unstuck and for helping individuals to identify and differentiate from the emotional lies that have ruled their life and influenced their decision-making. Under the pressure of real life, I have found a way through the use of the Core Story to open the door to a person's spiritual dimension. People need insight, understanding, knowledge, and a safe place to process their life's journey. I have experienced that when people are given good information, time, and safety, they can work through any life issue and trauma.

It has become evident to me that when people get serious about personal transformation, they benefit from committing to a regimen that reinforces their attempt to incorporate Core Truths to replace their Core Lies. This transformation process, as outlined by Don Crossland in the book cited previously, will need to center on the regular practice of these five steps:

1. REFRAME your faulty system of beliefs: recall all that you learned as a result of completing the Core Story process.
2. REBOND with the love that can heal: be willing to forgive yourself and move forward.
3. REANCHOR around Core Truths: make truth the target of your transformation journey.

4. REBUILD around appropriate boundaries: take respectful action and reconcile with others.
5. REPLACE Core Lies and refocus on Core Truths: reject the intrusion of your old ways of thinking as Core Lies will not be forgotten but can be overcome.

As my lifelong mentor and founder of Heartbeat, Inc., and current moderator of the website On Being Human, Landon Saunders, says, "There is nothing in the world more important than a human being." I stand amazed at the greatness of a person. This greatness is revealed as they learn to think and to believe in and to love themselves. I believe there is an invisible power in each person, and the Core Story awakens that dimension and a passion for life.

SECTION 3

Communication and Topics for Discussion

Sharing is a nutrient to being married; it is what keeps a couple sensitive and responsive to one another. – Ronald Joyner

CHAPTER 12

Good Communication Requires Flexibility

The purpose of this section is to provide an experiential element to the overview about being married provided in Section 1. We will distinguish five different phases of marriage, each with specific characteristics that will influence how couples relate to and communicate with one another at any particular point in time. Specific discussions will also be introduced that will focus attention on topics that will help couples gain insight into how they see themselves and each other. Not only will couples benefit from engaging in these fifty-two discussions on their own, but counselors, ministers, and life coaches will also find these discussions useful for making at-home assignments, planning a program of aftercare, or designing group workshop exercises.

Communication is as vital to relationships as blood is to the body. Lose too much blood and the body will die. Lose too much communication and the vitality of being married will disappear. Couples that don't know how to communicate with understanding will see their relationship wither away. Francis of Assisi said, "Seek first to understand and then to be understood."

> *Communication is as vital to relationships as blood is to the body.*

Being married is a very dynamic existence. The issues to be faced and the focus of communication will be different at different times. It is possible that meaningful communication will take place at one time but will be more difficult or stifled at another. In the discussions that are part of this section, four sequential stages of being married are identified—these are the Establishment Stage (years 1–7), Growth Stage (years 8–20), Transition Stage (years 21–35), and the Mature Stage (years 36 and beyond). These stages are related to the passage of time and are fixed as to when they will occur. These stages of being married move only in one direction: forward.

But within any stage of being married there can exist any one of five situational, developmental phases. The phase that a couple is in at any point in time is determined by how far along the developmental scale they are in processing the issues they are facing.

When involved in any of the fifty-two discussions presented in this section, it is easy to establish the stage based on how long a couple has been married. Determining what phase they are in may be more difficult.

Any one of these five phases in being married as developed by the authors can be experienced at any point in time, and a couple can be in different phases when dealing with different issues.

1. The Honeymoon Phase
2. The Awakening Phase
3. The Crucible Phase
4. The Silver Phase
5. The Golden Phase

The phases of being married are not ones to be passed through once and never repeated again. The developmental aspects of being married do not necessarily move along steadily and incrementally like the four stages of being married. Relationships can backslide, and new challenges can move a couple back to the starting line. Being married is a multi-layered phenomenon where different aspects of the relationship can be in different phases all at the same time.

Take a moment to study the characteristics of each of the five phases of being married:

The Honeymoon Phase: This is a phase in being married that can be characterized by words such as expectation, promise, excitement, progress, optimism, and adventure.

The Awakening Phase: This is a phase in being married that can be characterized by words such as awareness, listening, observing, accommodation, accountability, possibility, learning, adjusting, and difference.

The Crucible Phase: This is a phase in being married that can be characterized by words such as disappointment, hurt, discouragement, reconsideration, fear, blame, forgiveness, search, change, despair, confrontation, doubt, resolution, determination, failure, and hope.

The Silver Phase: This is a phase in being married that can be characterized by words such as understanding, discovery, acceptance, story, worth, direction, transformation, kindness, sharing, and overcoming.

The Golden Phase: This is a phase in being married that can be characterized by words such as unity, purpose, stamina, confidence, consistency, harmony, respect, stability, compatibility, and love.

Keep these phases in mind as you work through the fifty-two weekly conversations that are part of this section. Being aware of the psychodynamics involved with each phase will help you get more out of these discussions as well as help you better navigate your way through any points of disagreement or misunderstanding.

CHAPTER 13

Focused Communication Creates a Path for Mutual Understanding

The objective in providing these discussions is to provide good information and encouragement to couples who are married or giving consideration to being married, and who are seeking ways to better understand themselves and to share a meaningful life with one another. We have developed a series of fifty-two weekly messages for discussion to serve as a guide to help couples in their effort of self-discovery and in their attempt to better communicate with their spouse about important aspects of their relationship. These messages cover a wide range of topics and incorporate reading, meditation, and discussion as a way to enhance the conversation overall.

There is a presupposition that underlies each of these weekly messages. Time tested truth, which is being referred to as Core Truth, exists about how human beings can best relate to one another. We believe a reliable source for Core Truth is the Bible. For this reason, specific but optional passages from biblical Scripture will be provided under References and Endorsements at the end of this book in support of the fifty-two discussions.

Time tested truth, which is being referred to as Core Truth, exists about how human beings can best relate to one another.

Core Truth asserts that love is the driving force of life and the means by which we as human beings nurture one another. Nowhere is real love—

where the welfare of others is equal to what we desire for ourselves—more necessary or more evident than in being married. Nowhere is the way to love others better presented than in the Bible.

Sometimes Core Truth becomes obscured by what you may have come to believe about yourself and life in general. We have all developed controlling Core Beliefs about how to stay safe, how to be valued, and how to stay in control. Sometimes these Core Beliefs come out of bad information or from trauma, resulting in distorted views about self-preservation and limitations in the ability to judge the needs of others. Some of the experiences or impressions create what we have termed a Core Wound to the personality.

Left alone, a Core Wound can support a Core Lie which can distort relationships and cause a misinterpretation of life circumstances. Such a Core Lie can damage the ability of any of us to actually sense and appropriately respond to the needs of those around us. Persistent thoughts of being unworthy, under a threat, incapable, or undesirable (just to mention a few of the possibilities) can all result in troubled relationships because of an inaccurate self-perception and a false interpretation of how to best relate to others.

Left alone, a Core Wound can support a Core Lie which can distort relationships and cause a misinterpretation of life circumstances.

We hope that by working through the fifty-two weekly discussions couples can sort out and understand more about how their life views and personal beliefs are impacting their ability to understand and value one another. Also, being aware of the phase in being married as it relates to the topic being discussed will bring an added perspective as couples seek to meaningfully communicate with one another.

There may be a preference to group the reading or discussion of these messages by a common topic. If so, listed below are the ten general topic areas covered by the discussions:

1. Partnership: Weeks 3, 4, 5, 25, 40
2. Foundation: Weeks 8, 9, 10, 31, 46, 48
3. Communication: Weeks 7, 14, 16, 20, 41, 49
4. Compatibility: Weeks 17, 43, 44, 45, 47, 52
5. Conflict: Weeks 1, 2, 32, 34
6. Sex: Weeks 33, 35, 36, 37
7. Children: Weeks 21, 22, 23, 30, 38
8. Traits or Attributes: Weeks 11, 12, 24, 26, 39, 50
9. Wisdom: Weeks 13, 15, 27, 28, 51
10. Scriptural: Weeks 6, 18, 19, 29, 42

We also offer a few suggestions you might consider as you are working through each of these discussions. Set aside time each week to process each discussion topic. These steps can all be completed in one sitting or they can be accomplished at different times throughout the week. The following regimen may prove helpful.

Step 1: Read the message for the week and the related biblical passages, if you wish, listed under References and Endorsements at the end of the book.

Step 2: Meditate on the message and focus on what it is saying to you.

Step 3: Discuss the message along with your thoughts with your spouse.

Step 4: Journal your reflections about what you have learned.

Step 5: Think about how you might best incorporate what you have learned into your relationship.

Step 6: Commit yourself to implementing what you have learned.

Step 7: Celebrate life and being married with your spouse.

CHAPTER 14

Topics for Discussion

Constructive Confrontation

Being married is an emotionally charged relationship that comes with high—and oftentimes unrealistic—expectations. While high expectations can result in misunderstandings and hurt feelings, learning how to constructively push through these inevitable confrontations can become one of the keys to maintaining a fulfilling and joyful relationship.

Each person who enters into a marital relationship brings deeply held, often unconscious beliefs and expectations about what they need to feel safe and secure, to feel valued and loved, and to feel a sense of personal power and control.

When a person's unconscious, self-protecting beliefs and unrealistic expectations are driving their thoughts and actions, hurtful things can be said, and regrettable behavior can occur. When you or your spouse are being driven by unconscious beliefs and are reacting instead of listening and responding appropriately during a confrontation, trespasses and tension are bound to occur.

Experiencing conflict is a natural part of life. **Being married is an ideal setting for two individuals to engage in the constructive confrontations that will result in self-discovery and personal growth.** Being married can be one of the most enriching relationships on earth where a husband and wife can discover and process how their beliefs and behaviors are impacting the way they see and relate to themselves and others.

While it can be challenging to have a confrontation result in a constructive outcome, the time and effort invested toward this end will pay great dividends. Where else but within the covenant promise of a married relationship might there be the honest desire and commitment to intimately know, help, forgive, and carry on with another person despite the circumstances?

Being married is a gift because it is a vehicle for growth and maturity. It is where familiarity, proximity, frequency, and opportunity can operate in unison to reveal (and often heal) a person's Core Beliefs, expose Core Lies, heal Core Wounds, and discover Core Truths.

When a couple makes an honest effort to learn about their innermost thoughts, feelings, expectations, wounds, and sensitivities, they will experience the clarity, purpose, and harmony that will better equip them to cultivate and maintain an atmosphere of mutual understanding and compassion, which are some of the major ingredients to a long and satisfying relationship while being married.

Whose Truth?

A husband and wife each bring into their marital relationship Core Beliefs that have been depended upon to preserve their personal well-being and identity. A husband and wife also bring into their marital relationship different teachings and traditions that have been observed or passed on to them by their respective family, religion, community, etc.

At best, each spouse will bring into the relationship beliefs and habits that are honorable and that will benefit being married. At worst, there are behaviors and ways of thinking better abandoned or left in the past. Either way, personal habits and deeply ingrained elements of personality are not easily changed, abandoned, or altered without some degree of resistance.

So when a husband and wife encounter conflict over differing beliefs, traditions, or ways of thinking, whose truth wins? Is one spouse's experience more valid than the other's? Should one spouse simply defer to the other, or should each actively change their way of thinking about the matter at hand? These are all hard questions.

One of the first steps in resolving differing viewpoints requires each spouse to participate in active listening. Active listening requires there be no judgment placed on the spouse that is sharing. Active listening also requires that both spouses refrain from being defensive about parts of the conversation that apply directly to them.

The process of information gathering moves deeper when each spouse honestly and objectively observes how their words and actions affect their mate. Once each spouse recognizes and assumes personal responsibility for their actions, progress can be made in identifying common ground.

But active listening and close observation only go so far. **Finding trustworthy people and other sources of information about living with oneself and others can help bring objectivity and experience into the truth-seeking effort.** Seeking out successfully married couples, reading books, researching trusted online resources compiled by credentialed professionals, engaging in introspection that is guided by trained behavioral counselors, and meditating on biblical Scripture are all trustworthy sources for reliable information about better thinking, better living, and being a better companion.

Always keep this thought in mind: *It is important to remain emotionally open and available to the possibility that personal change may be necessary for you!*

WEEK 3

Partnership in Being Married

Being successful at being married is the result of forming a partnership where both the husband and wife not only share a common vision for the future but equally share in the benefits of the relationship.

Vision is a goal, a hope, an expectation. Vision is what you want to accomplish together. To be effective in achieving a vision, spouses must act in unison regarding the direction for being married.

Burdened with the liability of not sharing a common vision, being married can reach a destination for which neither partner is prepared. Married couples must commit to first establishing and then to sustaining a common vision for their life together.

Other liabilities in a marital partnership are emotional. Unlike a business partnership where shared liabilities involve money, paying down an emotional liability involves both partners "owning up" to their portion of what is due.

Where in business what is tendered to reduce a liability is cash, in a marital partnership the currency used is honesty, transparency, vulnerability, and forgiveness. Using this emotional currency, liabilities can be reduced while producing a dividend of trust and understanding.

Being in a partnership entails bearing an equal responsibility for any liabilities that exist. Not every couple will be able to reach on their own the level of self-awareness and mutual understanding that will be necessary to reduce or eliminate the liabilities in their marital partnership. They will need help. Where help is not required from professionals who can provide facilitated and therapeutic assistance, couples can confer with other couples who have mature and stable marital relationships. Other resources for self-help are listed under Reading Resources.

Planning for the Journey of Being Married

If you and your spouse are preparing for a long trip, there are some important things that need to be settled before you begin. What is the route to be taken? Is there enough room for the luggage? Where will you stay? How much can you afford to spend? Will there be stops or side trips along the way? A good trip begins with good preparation.

The journey of being married is no different. In order to enjoy the trip and ultimately reach your destination, you and your partner must communicate and coordinate. Things such as schedules, expenditures, chores, handling confrontation, allocation of personal time, raising and disciplining children, spiritual practices—these matters must be discussed so that a husband and wife are following the same route and have the same expectations about the destination of their relationship.

When taking a journey of any length or complexity, there likely will be detours, flat tires, bad weather, or stalled traffic. You can get hurt. This is also true in being married.

Trip guidance from above can help. **Navigation aids can speed a journey along by helping you identify hazards, plan alternate routes, and keep you from getting lost.** If you are in a car, this would be a GPS device; **in your marital relationship this would be relying upon good, time-tested, spiritually sound information.**

Let's not overlook driver fatigue! Sharing the driving on a long trip will make the journey safer and more enjoyable for everyone by allowing both occupants time to rest and enjoy the scenery. Both a husband and a wife need to share the load.

Good relationships are not the ones that experience no road hazards and no road fatigue. The best marital relationships are those that share in the driving and navigate with vigilance around what is difficult and unexpected.

WEEK 5

Giving and Receiving
While Being Married

In a healthy marital relationship, there is a balance of giving and receiving. When the balance of giving and receiving is not proportionate, there's the likelihood that unnecessary stress and unhappiness will occur.

For instance, think of a pond. When water flows into a pond more than it flows out, the pond may become stagnant, toxic, or full of sediment; it might even overflow and cause damage to its surroundings. More so, if the water flowing out of the pond is not adequately replenished, the pond may become dry and unable to provide in times of drought.

A solid marital relationship is one where the commitment to one another sees beyond whatever may be missing at the moment. Ideally, being married is a reciprocation of affection, respect, work, sharing, and fidelity, but this will not always be the case. There will be times in any relationship when one member of the couple will fail the other or when one partner will "carry" the other by "taking up the slack" either emotionally, financially, spiritually, or physically.

Giving is not just about buying something shiny or new for your partner. **The greatest forms of giving actually take place when you gift your partner with encouragement, affection, acknowledgment, comfort, and assistance. Giving also happens when you shower your partner with the gifts of forgiveness, compassion, respect**—and when you pardon your partner if they're having a crummy day.

It's also important to be aware that should you or your spouse become chronically needy or excessively benevolent, these extremes will not only affect the emotional ecology of being married but can dramatically affect the "give and take" balance that is needed for the maintenance of a healthy relationship.

WEEK 6

Being Married Is a Sacred Design

Being married is a sacred design. It is a magnificent institution and an intentional element within God's creation. Just as God knew we needed sunshine and rain to live, God also knew that the element of being married would be crucial to both the maintenance of a family unit and to the enhancement of personal development. **The marital relationship was intended to be an intimate and sacred space for men and women to live, love, mature, and procreate.**

The relational context for being married as ordained by God is so strong and binding that Christ's relationship with the church in Scripture is referred to as "bride and groom." And just as a relationship with Christ and the church enhance your life spiritually, being married is intended to produce and enhance your life relationally.

Being married was never intended to be a casual association between a man and a woman, rather this special relationship was designed to be the state of being for two people who have made a covenant pledge to remain together for a lifetime.

The binding of a man and a woman together in a stable family unit was part of God's initial creation, and just like the sun, the moon, the ocean, and the stars, the marital relationship remains in existence today.

Being married is like a mirror as each partner comes face-to-face with who they really are. Each partner comes face-to-face with their imperfections and the effects of their decisions and actions upon others.

The marital relationship is also like God's potter's wheel. God can be creative and innovative with those who are married by molding a couple who seeks his guidance into the real and relevant creatures he intends them to be.

WEEK 7

Why Is Being Married Easier for Some Couples?

Have you ever observed a married couple and wondered why their relationship appears to be so easy and happy and peaceful?

It's true that for some couples there is a natural rhythm and harmony that radiates from the relationship and makes their being married shine internally and externally. But what is the secret to those enviable relationships? Is it because the partners are just *compatible*? How do these couples make it look so easy? Maybe the answer lies with the fact that these couples possess some basic relational knowledge (and tools) for how to get along peacefully and joyfully, so they get off to a better start.

No matter what path a couple takes to reach harmony in their relationship, there's no question that being married requires a high level of mutual awareness and active participation by each partner. It's like being in a band. If you want your effort to produce good music, each member of the ensemble has to know, practice, and play the notes that will make a beautiful sound.

One characteristic of easier marital relationships is a commitment to be honest. When you commit to being honest, it allows you and your spouse to live in the reality of your circumstances. Being honest provides the foundation for trust. Honesty provides consistency; consistency provides stability; stability breeds confidence; confidence creates peace.

Another defining characteristic of easier marital relationships is humility. When you practice humility, it allows for you to acknowledge your flaws and understand how those flaws impact your partner. Practicing humility also equips you to make any personal changes that are necessary to strengthen being married. Humility never demands a winner or a loser. Rather, it demands that you confront yourself and your spouse in truth—which leads to healing, harmony, and happiness.

What's the Main Thing in Being Married?

Being married has a main thing. Maybe it's something really big or important that attracts a couple to one another and becomes the glue that holds them together. The main thing may be chemistry, lifestyle, socio-economics, faith, or familial obligation. But the big question to be answered is this: "Will what brought you together be able to keep you together?"

When you ask just about anyone why they marry, it's very likely that they will say it is because they are "in love." This is a very reasonable and understandable response! However, there's a deeper question: "Does this love sit on top of something else?"

What if a couple in love is getting married to satisfy family, cultural, or religious expectations? What if a couple in love wants children (or doesn't want children)? What if a couple in love is very concerned about economic security or financial success? What if the priority of a couple in love is maintaining sex appeal or a certain lifestyle?

The truth is that couples marry while they are "in love"—but very often there is a secondary objective for each partner that may be quite strong, pragmatic, and self-serving. Many people marry with a very specific outcome in mind. When their expectations are not met, they may lose their enthusiasm to continue in the relationship. (Statistically, this happens about 50 percent of the time to both Christians and non-Christians.)

When "the main thing" that draws a couple into being married goes away or is unable to be attained, what remains? Will the relationship still be meaningful enough and fulfilling to both the husband and the wife?

Being married is where both the husband and wife have made an unconditional commitment for each to act in the best interest of the other. For this to be possible, their **love must sit upon a foundation made up**

of respect, humility, honesty, singleness of purpose, personal growth, and forgiveness.

Where being married is viewed as a covenant, a husband and wife see each other as having significance and value even in the hardest of times. There will always be the desire to recognize, honor, and build up one another regardless of the challenges or circumstances.

The Foundation for Being Married

If you want to experience unity, both you and your marital partner must agree upon a set of principles that will guide and sustain your relationship through the many seasons of life. Both you and your partner must agree upon what the foundation of being married will be.

In selecting the principles that will guide you, it's important to be aware that there is a difference between opinion and truth. Opinions are like the wind. They are always shifting and can change in an instant due to error or misunderstanding. More so, opinions are ultimately self-serving notions that are unable to provide a sustainable foundation for life or for being married. As the saying goes, one person's opinion is often as good as another's!

If you and your partner truly want to experience unity and are seeking an unshakable foundation for your relationship, the Bible is a really good place to look for guidance. Not only does it reveal the truth about mankind, it provides insight and direction about being married.

Because being married was established by the Creator of mankind, it only makes sense that the information and knowledge needed about being married is to be found in the Creator's revelation to mankind, the Bible. This third-party truth, revealed to us and preserved over time through the oversight of the Holy Spirit, provides an incredible compass for navigating what is intended to be a lifelong relationship.

When both a husband and wife seek truth over opinion, consider biblically-based teachings over social trends, and have a shared commitment to studying the Bible, being married will not only be enriched and enlightened, but the foundation of the relationship will be more secure.

The Establishment Stage of Being Married

There are, for the purpose of these discussions, four stages of being married—the Establishment Phase (years 1–7), the Growth Stage (years 8–20), the Transition Stage (years 21–35), and the Mature Stage (years 36 and beyond). During the first seven years, the relationship transitions from wooing to doing. These are the years when the beautiful wrapping of the courtship is removed to discover what is inside the gift of being married.

Statistically, twenty percent of people will not like what they find during the first five years of being married and will divorce. This happens when newly married couples discover that traction is different from attraction. Many couples within this first stage of being married discover that working together presents much more of a challenge than merely being together. Dissatisfied with reality, they wish they could travel back in time to the ease of what things were like when they were dating. However, it's important to note that dating only presents the challenge of coordination. It is being married that presents the challenge (and rewards) of consolidation.

Being married needs to set on a solid, secure foundation that consists of shared guidelines for the relationship. Some of those guidelines are rooted in the commitment to listen, to learn, to adapt, to encourage, to serve, and to forgive. **When a marital relationship is built upon a solid and safe foundation, there is a framework for couples to practice being supportive, cooperative, consistent, dependable, trustworthy, even-tempered, attentive, and courteous.**

Just as no person is born knowing how to speak in full sentences—no person is born knowing how to be married. Being married is a skill that is learned and practiced over time. More so, this complex relationship is not the fulfillment of a storybook illusion. Nor, is it about reproducing what your parents had (or didn't have).

If a couple can make it through the establishment phase of being married, learn how to process their own stuff, and move intentionally and compassionately through life with their spouse, each partner will not only be made more whole as a person, but being married will be made stronger through the process.

Trust Is a Must

Being able to trust your partner is one of the most important ingredients for sustaining a healthy and joyful marital relationship. Having trust is like having clean air to breathe; it is life-giving. It helps maintain the vitality of being together and provides the security and confidence that is necessary for a couple to commit to and be forgiving of one another.

When you are able to trust your partner, it creates a feeling of safety and the space for each of you to be vulnerable and transparent. When there is no vulnerability or transparency, there is likely to be only a very shallow and cautious relationship.

Having a firm foundation of trust makes it possible to extend the benefit of the doubt when your spouse's words or actions are out of character. Trust serves as a buffer that can temper the reflex to jump to a negative conclusion when something troubling happens before all the facts are known.

Trust is the framework around which hope is built, and hope is the emotional fuel that keeps being married a growing and progressing experience.

Trust emerges from a set of beliefs about your spouse, and when these beliefs are shattered it becomes difficult to know what can be depended upon. The process of rebuilding trust in being married is a challenge. It requires time and patience, forgiveness, and grace. It requires one spouse (whose trust has been broken) to be willing to once again trust in the other. It requires overcoming skepticism about ever being able to trust your spouse again because doubt is the scar left by a breach of trust.

A Laboratory for Grace

Being married serves many purposes. Not only is this a sacred setting designed for partners to experience intimate companionship, sexual expression, child rearing, and sharing in the work that makes up daily living—it is also an extraordinary laboratory for grace. This setting allows us to learn, on a daily basis, how to get along with others and how to practice forgiveness regarding the shortcomings of another.

Grace is the offering of unmerited favor to others, and it should be the by-product of the love that a married couple has for one another. Grace is the relational lubricant that helps keep the wheels of being married from squeaking. There is no other setting in life (maybe with the exception of being part of the crew of a submarine or one of the astronauts in the International Space Station) where the proximity between two people requires as much forbearance—for the sake of maintaining a workable, productive, and enjoyable coexistence.

There are also few relationships in life where a person can be hurt as badly as in being married. Even when fault is admitted and forgiveness is sought for a major breach of the marital covenant, extending grace to the offending spouse can be very difficult. It takes a lot of soul searching to be able to rekindle the desire to rebuild an intimate relationship that has been fractured.

Extending grace to another doesn't mean that you are adopting a passive or permissive attitude. It merely means that others don't have to be without fault to be valued and honored. Grace does not require you to compromise what is right; instead, grace is in evidence when you choose to forgive, adapt, and move forward. **Grace embraces the idea that forgiveness, following genuine remorse, can actually contribute to the realization of a greater good.**

Choosing to practice grace helps nurture, repair, and sustain being married. Forgiveness interrupts what might otherwise result in a tragic and destructive cycle of accusation, retribution, and alienation.

A Source for Wisdom in Being Married

Some of the factors contributing to being better at being married are obvious while others are not. These elusive elements are just as important as the obvious ones.

Every person, regardless of their religious beliefs or inclinations, can benefit in being married if they are familiar with or persuaded by biblical instructions about relationships. Wisdom is found in Scripture, and wisdom acts as an unseen hand in helping a person navigate life.

There is also a fuller measure of this unseen hand for every married Christian. This unseen hand is a part of the gift that every Christian receives when obediently acknowledging Jesus as the Son of God and accepting his dominion over the way life is to be lived.

The spiritual connection that the Holy Spirit provides to the receptive believer improves insight into the will of God and stimulates the desire to live selflessly and lovingly with others. This gift of the Holy Spirit of God is the fresh relational air breathed by those who want to be spiritually alive and who through faith strive for fulfillment in all aspects of life.

If the Holy Spirit seems elusive and mysterious, that's because this is the nature of the Holy Spirit. The Spirit is unseen, yet ever present. The Spirit is influential without being coercive. The Holy Spirit works to protect and enrich because it is the intention of God that being married be a blessing in the lives of both the husband and the wife.

Practicing Being Present

Being present as a spouse means so much more than just being home every night for dinner. It means more than just sleeping in the same bed, attending the same functions, and helping with household duties.

Being present is listening, processing, and responding attentively in real-time. Responses can then be centered on what is actually going on at the time and what is most needed in the moment by your partner.

Being present is more than just paying attention. Being present requires that a couple genuinely be tuned-in to what is being said and to what is going on. **Being present allows room for a fresh interpretation of otherwise familiar statements or situations based upon newly relevant information.**

Being present with another takes extra time and a concerted effort, as countless distractions and interruptions compete for our attention throughout each day. This approach to being attentive to your spouse will pay off big time as you become more sensitive and supportive.

Staying present with one another is one surefire way for a couple to accurately, consistently hear and respond to one another appropriately.

It's All about You!

Wouldn't it be great and so much easier if being married was only centered around you and your needs? Well, believe it or not, being married really is all about you! However, it's not exactly what you may be thinking or hoping for!

The truth is, being married is all about you coming face-to-face with who you really are and learning how to make the necessary adjustments to become the best life partner you can be.

Coming face-to-face with who we really are and taking responsibility for all of our behavior (positive and negative) is not easy. It takes time to come to terms with who we really are because looking in the mirror isn't always pretty, especially if we operate from a self-focused perspective.

Fortunately, being married is intended to be a long-lasting relationship that provides plenty of time for coming to terms with who you are—and time for making any necessary adjustments. Given the proximity of living with another person on a day-to-day basis, the accountability that this arrangement requires, and the familiarity that being married breeds, this sacred relationship was created to reveal and challenge the truest parts of ourselves.

Coming face-to-face with ourselves is scary and risky and challenging. And once a person reaches adulthood, it can be more difficult to change—that is, to finish growing up. Being married involves maturing, but in a different (and more fulfilling) way. It's about learning, listening, adapting, and changing in an effort to become the best version of you. It's about transforming in front of your partner's eyes and being okay with revealing all the best and worst parts of yourself.

WEEK 16

Listening for Learning

Hearing someone and listening to someone are two different actions. The act of hearing is the recognition that someone is speaking. The act of listening is being attentive to what is being said.

Listening is much more important than hearing. For instance, when you truly listen to your marital partner, you will wait until they are finished sharing to begin your reply. You will also refrain from drawing a conclusion before your partner has finished sharing.

When you decide to be an active listener, it creates an atmosphere of empathy with your spouse. **And when you pay attention to the details and nuances of what is being said—you become more aware of what is being shared at the innermost level and at the root of your partner's concern.**

If you are disinterested, distracted, self-defensive, or presumptuous when your partner is sharing, these behaviors can create barriers to listening. And if you really want to reply to your partner with love and compassion, listening is the prerequisite to any meaningful response. Careful listening is a gift you give to your partner, who desires and deserves to be heard.

Sometimes listening is difficult because you may have an apprehension about dealing with what your partner is sharing. In this case, rather than tuning your partner out, share with your partner how difficult it is for you to process what is being shared.

There are also instances when your partner wants to talk about something that you have no particular interest in. In this case, it's important to make the effort to lend your time and your ear to your partner which will ensure your partner does not feel discounted or ignored.

While communication issues are one of the most common and frequent complaints made by both husbands and wives, if you want to improve and enhance being married, commit to really listening to your partner and experience how rewarding this can be for both of you!

Happiness: It's Up to You

If you were to ask your friends, family, and partner if they want to be happy, most everyone would answer, "Yes!" Personal happiness is a very natural and common desire.

It is great when one spouse is supportive of the things that are fulfilling to the other, but this is not always possible. When this support does not occur, it's important for each marital partner to understand that their personal happiness is not dependent on their being married or on their spouse.

If you are looking to experience a stable and sustainable relationship, it's important to realize that your personal happiness is not the responsibility of your spouse. You are responsible for your own happiness regardless of what your spouse does or does not do.

If you are happy when you are with your spouse, that is wonderful! But, if you are not happy when you are with your spouse, it's not always due to your partner. This to say, it is unrealistic if you are depending upon your spouse to make you feel happy. Even the best spouse fails from time to time in meeting their partner's needs or expectations.

Furthermore, it's important to stay away from the blame-game when it comes to your feelings of happiness and contentment. If you blame your partner for your unhappiness, it can do real harm to your relationship and breed resentment.

The balance for a husband and wife to seek is creating an atmosphere of mutual nurturing while at the same time strengthening individual identities. A healthy awareness of self creates a path for each partner to establish a sense of well-being that is not dependent upon what the other spouse provides.

Love at its best provides a couple an element of trust that allows personal independence without sacrificing the sense of togetherness which is so important to the experience of being married.

Biblical Teaching on Being Married (Part 1)

Over time and human history, the Bible has proven to be a reliable source of good information. It teaches us about how to live life with integrity, how to love one another, and it even shares information about how to be an honorable and loving spouse.

While the Bible can sometimes be difficult to understand and at times seem irrelevant to modern times, its truths are timeless and its instruction on how to love others is crucial to living life to the fullest.

When you look to the Bible for information, it depicts being married in two ways. It depicts it as a relationship characterized by equality and reciprocation. It also depicts it as a relationship where there is male headship.

These depictions of being married have served both as rally cries for those espousing male supremacy and for those championing a totally egalitarian relationship. **Yet, the real meaning for being married is best obtained by a loving and mutually considerate blending of the various views portrayed in biblical texts.**

When a married couple commits to studying the Bible and its teachings (on all areas of life), there are insights and revelations that occur. And when a balanced and biblical perspective is developed between you and your spouse, the fruits of peace and companionship will abound!

No matter which way you look at it, being married is a complex human relationship. It can be as difficult to describe as the awe one experiences when witnessing the vastness of the Grand Canyon. That is, being married can no more be described from a single segment of Scripture than the Grand Canyon can be described from only one overlook.

As you and your spouse continue to build a deeper understanding of your relationship, there may be differing views and interpretations of Scripture. Even so, dwell first and foremost on learning how to love one another.

Biblical Teaching on Being Married (Part 2)

If there's one thing you and your spouse can easily agree on—it's the simple fact that being married is complex. It is a relationship that requires effort! And, if you've been married for any length of time, you probably can also agree that a healthy relationship must be more than just a replication of your parents' relationship or a fulfillment of society's expectations.

If you and your spouse are looking to gain a better understanding of what it takes to have a healthy relationship, the Bible can be a great resource and starting point. When both you and your partner allow Scripture to speak as "this *and* that" rather than "this *or* that," you are creating the necessary space to honor being together for the intricate bond that it is. Simply put, when you or your partner select a single Scripture to define being married, this forces an exclusivity of meaning that will deny the rich, multi-dimensional consideration that your relationship deserves.

As with any healthy relationship, being married requires relational balance. Whether the issue is submission, intimacy, recreation, parental discipline, finances, in-laws, church life, or wall colors—the balance between dominance and deference is critical if your goal is to maintain a win-win atmosphere for both you and your spouse.

Following the adage, "Everyone has their say, but not everyone has their way" works as long as "has their way" works as evenly as the chance of getting heads on the toss of a coin.

Being married is complex. It is the theatre where day-by-day we play out both the heart-rending and the heart-warming saga of the battle between cooperation and self-determination, between looking toward heaven and being earth-bound. Not even the inspired writers of the Bible could reduce this drama down to a single scene.

The Growth Stage of Being Married

There are, for the purpose of these discussions, four stages of being married—the Establishment Phase (years 1–7), the Growth Stage (years 8–20), the Transition Stage (years 21–35), and the Mature Stage (years 36 and beyond). While many couples may feel quite comfortable during the Growth Stage of being married, it is within these years that some of the most profound personal and relational growth occurs.

Wouldn't it be great if after the first seven years of being married both you and your partner's bad habits disappeared? And all of the incorrect information you brought into the relationship was corrected? And all the mistakes you both have made were overcome and forgiven? And both of you had reached a complete understanding of one another?

Well, this just doesn't happen! Being married is a continuing developmental process, not a destination. However, with each new insight, with each good day, with each achievement—there is cause for celebration as the relationship grows.

It is during the Growth Stage of being married that the previous patterns of communication and decision-making (those that were developed during the first seven years) will be tested and refined. The challenges as well as the opportunities for growth during this stage will come from how matters are handled related to raising children, managing finances, making career choices and moves, and growing spiritually.

When trouble does raise its ugly head, effective conflict resolution will be especially important after being together longer because the stakes will be much higher and the losses can be so much greater.

During the Growth Stage of being married, hopefully both husband and wife will continue to gain insight into how much of their time, energy, and attention are being given over to self-will and self-need, and how much of their efforts are being directed toward responding to what is best for one another and the other members of the family.

WEEK 21

Children and Being Married (Part 1)

If you and your spouse have children, you know that becoming parents involves a huge transition. You also know that when you become a parent, the ways in which you parent your child serve as a relational magnifying glass. Because parenting is rarely easy and places many demands on a person, it has a way of amplifying both you and your spouse's positive and negative traits.

While children are a great blessing while being married, they can also be a major source of stress (even when things are going well)! **Your fears and apprehensions about yourself, your spouse, and your children surface as you carry out your childrearing responsibilities.**

For instance, if there are unresolved issues surrounding money, self-esteem, sex, relatives, religion, or career, these issues will seem larger due to the challenges inherent in raising children. More so, parenting children awakens attitudes, habits, and emotions reflective of the parents' experiences within their own families. Sometimes these awakenings may not be appropriate for the family of which these parents are now a part.

When any good thing in life arrives, it always presents opportunities and challenges. When you have children, you are given the special opportunity to help guide and train a person to live a life of truth, compassion, and relevance. Yet, the accompanying challenge is for both parents to channel the stress of raising children into an opportunity for their own personal growth and honing their cooperative skills.

Children and Being Married (Part 2)

Children are not busts to be sculpted into the image of their parents. From the moment a child enters into a couple's life, the mutual goal of the parents should be to prepare the child to eventually leave home as an independent, well-rounded, and self-defined individual. Every child deserves their own personhood.

While a child bears the genetic signatures of the parents, each child deserves more than becoming a clone of the parents. **Every child is the parents' opportunity to contribute a unique individual to the world, not just a duplicate of themselves or a fulfillment of their own unmet dreams.**

If parents are committed to the goal of helping their children develop into their own personhood, then parents must be open to the influence that time, talent, and circumstances will have upon the plans for their children.

Being committed to the process of parenting rather than the outcome of parenting will be one of the greatest gifts you give your child. When you are committed to the process, rather than the outcome, you acknowledge and create the needed space for possibility and discovery. You also help encourage and appreciate the uniqueness of the child.

When it comes to the responsibility of parenting, faith, not fear, should always drive your actions. Nurturing a child in a way that honors personhood will produce an outcome in adulthood that both fits the needs of the child and honors the efforts of the parents.

Children and Being Married (Part 3)

It is very common to experience differences in opinion with your spouse about parenting. It is also very common to experience conflict when there are strong differences of opinion on any subject. However, no matter how strong the differences of opinion are, the result of the conflict doesn't have to be a win-lose outcome. Neither you nor your spouse are in a losing position when the ultimate decision and the manner in which a decision is reached are in the best interest of the child.

In fact, when a child witnesses their parents engage in respectful disagreement, it can be instructive and educational. When you and your spouse make a decision that is mutually supported and suspends further disharmony, it creates an atmosphere of respect and peace in your home.

Seeing effective conflict resolution modeled at home is a great learning experience for children. **While the child may not always understand the complexities of their parents' disagreements, they will observe and record how each conflict is handled and ultimately resolved.**

When a child is exposed to differing points of view from their parents about one of their own life issues, a lesson takes place. In this situation, a child can see that an issue affecting their life can be viewed from different and mature perspectives.

Learning that there are alternatives available for the successful solution of a problem may literally be a life saver for a young person. Being exposed to critical thinking and problem solving can be a valuable gift parents give to their children.*

*Note: For this desired learning to ultimately take place, parents must openly and candidly communicate with their children the factors considered in making decisions about matters affecting their children's lives.

Laughter: The Best Medicine

Can you remember the last time you laughed together with your spouse? One of the most healing balms in life is laughter. When you and your spouse can see the humor in things that happen, you are both cultivating a valuable tool to be used in your relationship as well as practicing a healthy method of relieving stress and tension.

Humor is often experienced when the unexpected happens. It may be actions that exaggerate the most characteristic attributes of your spouse. It may be the recognition of the absurdity of what was expected (as compared to what actually happened). When you or your spouse don't take yourself too seriously—that's when you can experience the many benefits of humor.

Being able to embrace the humor in a situation can recalibrate the expectations of a husband and wife into a viewpoint that may be more real and reasonable.

Being able to see the humor in life and in being married is renewing, refreshing, and redemptive. A good laugh that is free from ridicule and not used as a way to avoid hard emotional work can be a great reminder that life is not perfect, people are not perfect, and circumstances are often out of our control.

The next time you and your spouse need to decompress after some type of mishap or disappointment, look for the humor. Humor is a compassionate and low-key way of processing unexpected outcomes without being caustic or dismissive. And it is one way of recognizing a need for change without being confrontational, especially when you are laughing together.

WEEK 25

Being Married as Teamwork

Being married is a unique and intimate relationship; however, it is not so unique that the concepts applicable to other group endeavors cannot be applied. Simply put, while it may be easy to compartmentalize our thinking about being married, **we must be aware that if we want to build a healthy and productive relationship, understanding the dynamics and importance of teamwork is crucial.**

Similar to functioning within a workplace team, you and your spouse need to first be unified by shared core values. Secondly, you and your spouse must learn how to establish the ground rules for decision-making. Thirdly, it is important that the goal and purpose of what issue is being decided upon is aligned between each spouse.

More so, there needs to be a mutual accountability where you and your spouse communicate freely in evaluating results against goals, identifying opportunities for improvement, and celebrating achievements. This interaction is best experienced when it takes place within an atmosphere of mutual respect and transparency (as openness, honesty, and collaboration build commitment and trust).

When there is a shared vision, open communication, and honesty among team members—the chances for success in the workplace greatly improve. And when you and your teammate (spouse) apply these same principles to being married, you will experience greater satisfaction and create space for greater joy, peace, and fulfillment.

WEEK 26

Vulnerability in Being Married

If you were to evaluate the healthy and happy aspects of being married, you would find several key ingredients: mutual respect, trust, and support. Yet, another key ingredient that is sometimes overlooked is vulnerability. Vulnerability is the willingness to share feelings, as well as talk about facts.

When there is vulnerability, you are able to be open with your spouse about your faults, dreams, and the personal doubts and aspirations you have concerning yourself and being married.

Just as trust and respect should be ground rules for being married, so should vulnerability. **When you nurture vulnerability, it helps create an atmosphere of tenderness, understanding, and intimacy.** Being vulnerable with your spouse says that you trust them and value their feedback. Being vulnerable is an emotional gift from one spouse to the other.

However, what you must guard against when your spouse is being vulnerable is any tendency to use what has been revealed in confidence as a weapon to make a point or win an argument. If you engage in this kind of behavior, the transparency and candor will disappear, and you may find your spouse embracing secrets. And when there are secrets between you and your spouse, they will eat away at the fabric of your relationship.

Being vulnerable with your spouse is a vital and delicate tool for building a healthy and happy relationship. And because vulnerability is the language of intimacy, it is a key ingredient if you and your spouse desire to establish authenticity and truthfulness as an integral part of being married.

WEEK 27

Wisdom from 350 Years of Being Married (Part 1)

Fourteen people came together for a brainstorming session to identify some of the factors that contribute to building and maintaining success in being married. Both men and women participated in this brainstorming session, and all participants were either currently married or married in the past.

Together, this group represented 350 years of experience in being married. Listed below are eleven of the twenty-two observations coming from this group:

1. Don't assign fault when trying to solve a problem.
2. When a problem is hard to solve, take the long view.
3. The approach to a disagreement must never be to win at any cost.
4. Don't dramatize problems or over-play your point of view.
5. Look at being married as a journey with turns.
6. After getting married, flirting with others is over.
7. One of the best ways to assist communication is to pray together.
8. Work to keep first things first; prioritize problems and issues by significance.
9. Balance the need for personal and together time.
10. Don't involve your parents in your disagreements.
11. Work on your friendship as well.

These observations are not being presented as a relational checklist, rather to illustrate some points to be considered when seeking to be better at being married.

WEEK 28

Wisdom from 350 Years of Being Married (Part 2)

Fourteen people came together for a brainstorming session to discuss the various factors that contribute to building and maintaining success in being married. Both men and women participated in this brainstorming session, and all participants were either currently married or married in the past.

Together, this group represented 350 years of experience in being married. Listed below are the last of the twenty-two observations coming from this group:

12. You will carry, and you will be carried at times while being married.
13. Your word should be your bond.
14. Never trash your mate to someone who is not your confidant.
15. Don't try to fix your spouse.
16. Devise temporary "get away" strategies for when things reach an impasse.
17. Consider the impact your actions and decisions will have on your spouse and children.
18. Consider the impact of the family of origin upon both you and your spouse.
19. Listen more than you talk.
20. Denial does not work. Deal with conflicts sooner rather than later.
21. Identify your gods (recognition, sports, work, etc.) and don't let them distract you from the needs of the relationship with your spouse.
22. Learn the difference between support and codependency or enabling.

These observations are not being presented as a relational checklist, rather to illustrate some points to be considered when seeking to be better at being married.

Being Married and Paul's Letter to the Philippians

No matter what you might believe and regardless of whether you are single or married, the Bible is a time-tested source of wisdom if you are seeking to live a peaceful, relevant, and meaningful life.

If you have spent any time looking in the Bible, you have encountered the writings of the apostle Paul who was one of Jesus' followers. In a message that Paul sent to a group of believers in the ancient city of Philippi (located in what is now the Macedonian area of eastern Greece), you will find some good information about what it takes to maintain a good relationship with others.

The Bible is a reliable document and worthy of consideration when choosing how to best live with other people, regardless of your spiritual orientation. Consider the following points contained in Paul's letter which can be applied even today to the relational aspects of being married.

"And this is my prayer: that your love may abound more and more in knowledge and depth of insight, so that you may be able to discern what is best and may be pure and blameless . . . ." Philippians 1:9–10

"Do nothing out of selfish ambition or vain conceit, but in humility consider others better than yourselves. Each of you should look not only to your own interests, but also to the interests of others." Philippians 2:3–4

"Do everything without complaining or arguing, so that you may become blameless and pure." Philippians 2:14–15

"Let your gentleness be evident to all. The Lord is near. Do not be anxious about anything, but in everything, by prayer and petition, with thanksgiving, present your requests to God. And the peace of God, which transcends all understanding, will guard your hearts and your minds in Christ Jesus." Philippians 4:5–8

"Finally, brothers, whatever is true, whatever is noble, whatever is right, whatever is pure, whatever is lovely, whatever is admirable, if anything is excellent or praiseworthy, think about such things." Philippians 4:8

WEEK 30

The Transition Stage of Being Married

There are for the purpose of these discussions four stages of being married—the Establishment Phase (years 1–7), the Growth Stage (years 8–20), the Transition Stage (years 21–35), and the Mature Stage (years 36 and beyond). The Transition Stage of being married is the stage when some or all of the children have left home, and work-life may have peaked.

At this point, a couple is typically looking forward to enjoying the fruits of their labor and the fulfillment that comes from having achieved and endured much together. This is also the period of time when marital partners can experience a personal and spiritual void. Because of this transitional challenge, this is often a time requiring personal reflection and seeking wisdom from outside sources.

During the Transition Stage of being married, a husband and wife might need to rediscover their identity and worth apart from parenthood or their career. This is an extremely valuable time for a couple as they each get back in touch with themselves and with each other. It is a time for a husband and wife to re-examine and recommit to the foundational truths of life and the basics of their relationship as a couple.

Couples who have neglected their own personal development or have let life pull them apart may experience during these transitional years what is often called a "mid-life crisis." This is a situation where "me" can destroy "we." At best, the transitional years are a time when married couples can reaffirm that they still need each other and can joyfully recommit to their covenant of being married.

The Transition Stage of being married is a time for rejuvenation, not stagnation; it is a time for establishing a renewed, and sometimes revised, vision for a future together.

Managing Your Emotions

Emotions are generated by beliefs. Whether we recognize it or not, many of our beliefs are formed from prejudiced and preconditioned points of view. This is why some of the biggest challenges faced by married couples are often the result of misunderstood and out-of-control emotions fueled by faulty beliefs.

As committed marital partners, you and your spouse must make an effort to develop an awareness about your emotions. **By developing a deeper awareness of your emotions and what beliefs and circumstances trigger your behaviors and reactions, you will be able to more appropriately respond to your partner with sensitivity and grace.**

Being married is not a refuge where one can live a sheltered, unchallenged life and remain *just the way I am*. It takes effort and patience to learn how to best express your emotions. Likewise, when negative situations arise, partners cannot just walk away or ignore what is happening. For instance, one spouse cannot create an emotional mess and expect the other spouse to clean everything up.

It is the intimacy and proximity that is sought in being married that also acts as the spotlight to illuminate emotional shortcomings. A husband and wife are forced to literally live with the results of their misspoken words, one-sided attitudes, misconceptions, and immaturities.

A husband and wife must each take the time, have the courage, and exercise the humility to examine the root of their emotions and how their personal beliefs affect their own life view and the well-being of those around them.

Making Things Worse

When you or your marital partner overreact to a problem, you can potentially do more damage to the relationship than the problem itself. Whenever there is difficulty, a door must be left open for the entry of remorse and reform. Retaliation does not create a path toward reconciliation, unless the objective is punishment rather than recovery.

Confronting an offense by your partner or letting your partner suffer the consequences of their actions are appropriate. However, what is counterproductive is when you continue to accuse, berate, demean, humiliate, set an unreasonably high bar for forgiveness, or remain punitive in every interaction.

These types of reactions to conflict do not leave room for a change of heart. Because whenever there is judgment there is also a sentence, and where there is a sentence there will be punishment. **An atmosphere of hostility is toxic to any attempt for honest resolution, for reconciliation, and for the maintenance of a viable marital relationship.**

While forgiving does not always equate to forgetting, transparency and accountability are always considered good medicines to treat the damage done when trust and security have been violated. Continuing to rub a spouse's nose in a transgression where there has been a genuine expression of sorrow may end up the biggest transgression of all!

Unfaithfulness in Being Married

When you think of unfaithfulness in being married, what probably comes to mind is the act of one partner committing adultery and breaking the sacred bond of physical intimacy. While this is indeed an act of unfaithfulness, being unfaithful can mean so much more than just sexual infidelity.

Actually, **unfaithfulness in being married is any act that undermines the covenant promise to be committed to working together for the mutual good of the partnership.** It might be verbal or physical abuse, deceitfulness, addiction, carelessness with money, spiritual callousness, neglect, unavailability, or vindictiveness—these are all ways that unfaithfulness can creep in and rob a relationship of peace and joy.

It is statistically proven that religious couples divorce at a rate similar to that of non-religious couples. This is because marital unfaithfulness, in all of its forms, is prevalent among believers and nonbelievers alike and has the same effect on religious couples as on non-religious couples. Just because a couple is not committing adultery does not mean that either or both spouses are not being unfaithful in other ways to the meaning and intent of being married.

If an expanded view of marital unfaithfulness is accepted and applied, then couples can become even more focused on avoiding ways of speaking and acting that are not good for building up and supporting one another.

The Goal Is Reconciliation

In any long-term relationship, from time to time there will be disagreements, even fierce arguments. However, the end-goal of any conflict should be resolution and reconciliation, not a big win.

When a spouse is focused on victory only, they are in essence demanding that they be deemed the winner and their spouse the loser. But, focusing on victory alone in an argument is counter-productive as it only fulfills the ego needs of one spouse, without counting the emotional and relational cost upon the other spouse.

In being married, a no-fault approach to conflict resolution is a much more productive strategy. In a no-fault approach, the goal in a disagreement is to find an answer that will resolve the point of contention and move both parties as quickly as possible toward a spirit of goodwill and good humor.

Simply put, if you and your spouse can adopt a no-fault approach, the goal will always be to agree on what is right, rather than on who is right. When tempers are heated and words are flying, a path must always be kept open for compromise, retreat, apology, or simply agreeing to disagree.

The commitment to be married should entail the commitment to create an atmosphere of peace. And if peace becomes absent through conflict, the goal then should be to restore the peace.

While it is possible (through personal and spiritual discipline) to cultivate individual peace in almost any circumstance, maintaining peace while being married requires practicing a no-fault approach when conflict arises, and making a commitment to being a peacemaker rather than a "winner."

What Sex While Being Married Is Not (Part 1)

Sex is *one* of the greatest gifts of being married, but it is not *the* greatest gift. It is intended for pleasure, building intimacy, and has the purposes of recreation, affirmation, and procreation. However, as a married person, it is important to understand that sex is not intended to be the basis of your identity or to serve as the defining point of your relationship.

Even in the best times, sexual performance will wax and wane. Being married and expecting you and your spouse's sexual performance to always be the same or the same as when you first got married are unrealistic expectations.

While the heat of passion for newlyweds can be intense, things as simple as fatigue, diet, age, pregnancy, or a new baby can alter the landscape of your sexual life. Furthermore, when the act of sex is misunderstood or overrated, it can weaken or destroy the enjoyment of being together.

It is only when the act of sex is treated with realistic expectations that it can be a reinforcing rather than a disappointing element of being married. Ultimately, every married person should understand that personal worth is so much more than the ability to have sex. Should disease, physiology, separation, or life circumstances create a physical challenge, no person is less of a man or a woman if they become impaired in regard to expressing themselves sexually. Loving, showing intimacy, and being a friend and faithful companion is what the real focus of being married should be.

What Sex While Being Married Is Not (Part 2)

The Bible teaches that sex is to be experienced within the safety and sanctity of the covenant of being married. This teaching is intended for each person's good and for the health of the relationship. And where sex can be a strong force and motivator for getting married, sex should not be allowed to be its defining aspect.

Relationship is what defines being married, not sex. Sexual intimacy is created to be only one component of the very multi-layered and complex relationship between a husband and wife.

The relationship of being married was created so that men and women do not have to be alone if they desire an intimate relationship. It was also designed to be a relationship that can create, protect, and nurture children. **While sex should be an affirmation of the marital relationship, it should never be allowed to define the sum and substance of what the relationship is all about.**

Of all human relationships, being married is unique as it involves four types of love—friendly, romantic, familial, and unconditional. It is only in this context where all of these aspects of love coexist and interplay with one another.

Erotic love and sex can be powerful forces and sources of energy for a married couple. Yet, sex alone should not be allowed to define the quality of the relationship, nor should sexual difficulties be allowed to diminish other aspects of intimate expression and marital joy.

What Sex While Being Married Is Not (Part 3)

Good sex is no guarantor of compatibility for an unmarried couple, and it is no proof of commitment or fidelity for those who are married. **Too many times the sex act is misinterpreted or given undeserved prominence in both dating and in being married.**

Because sex is such a powerful physical and emotional expression, it is often employed or interpreted, either consciously or unconsciously, to be the substance or benchmark of a meaningful interpersonal relationship between a man and a woman.

When sexual intercourse is understood properly, it becomes a marital gift intended to build intimacy and reaffirm genuine feelings between spouses. It reaffirms feelings of safety, truthfulness, desirability, vulnerability, affection, value, compatibility, and commitment. This intimate expression can be a powerful reinforcement of a covenant relationship. Where this is not the case, the act of sexual intercourse is little more than a loyalty test, or an act performed to control, to pleasure, or to exploit.

Simply, sex can be fickle. It can be inconsistent or great or difficult. What is most important for each spouse to understand is that sex is just one part of a larger whole. It is an aspect of being married that can bring either great joy or significant challenges.

Finding the Value in Being Married

There are many different things that bring value to being married. Education, career, financial security, children, and social position are just a few examples. These things can all bring a sense of well-being and accomplishment to the family.

Every couple should seek to add value to being married. However, there is nothing that brings a greater sense of well-being or accomplishment to a relationship than a husband and wife who discover the personal worth that each brings to being married.

If you want to learn how to truly value your spouse, it begins with learning how to treat them with compassion and to always act with their best interest in mind. **If you want to value your spouse, it will require you to consistently nurture them toward constructive ends without worrying whether you will benefit or not.** It will require you to do no harm and to continually extend compassion, forgiveness, encouragement, and protection. It will require that you learn how to offer constructive, respectful correction.

If there is contempt or a lack of mutual respect in being married, this attitude will hinder the ability to build a stable, mutually edifying relationship. The mutual acknowledgment by a couple of each other's personal worth is the foundation of a lasting and fulfilling marital relationship.

WEEK 39

Peace While Being Married

Peace in life and in being married can be found. Peace is a state of mind. A unique depth of peace can be experienced by those who identify as Christians and place their faith in Jesus Christ. This special peace is the presence and work of the Holy Spirit. The Holy Spirit is not just a "church thing" or "religious fiction." The Holy Spirit is God's actual presence in the life of a believer, and it is intended to be a source of wisdom, guidance, and comfort in any situation.

The peace that the Holy Spirit brings is what the apostle Paul refers to in the New Testament in Philippians 4:7 when he talks about a peace that "passes all understanding." And the Good News is that this special guiding and comforting presence is available to believers in all aspects of their life, including in being married.

There's no question that everyone faces times of trouble and fear. **However, for Christians, when times of trouble or fear are experienced, the Holy Spirit can be sought for insight, comfort, and direction.** Whether facing a personal temptation, a difficult decision, a health concern, or a professional challenge—God's spiritual presence only awaits our invitation.

And when there is a great challenge in being married, the Holy Spirit is always available and ready to comfort, guide, and bring peace. In fact, the Holy Spirit should be the first stop on a Christian believer's path to resolving conflict, seeking answers, or finding shelter in the midst of a bad situation.

When you and your spouse have a believing Christian faith and are able to trust in and rely on the Holy Spirit's intervention in times of difficulty, you are opening the door for the peace that "passes all understanding."

WEEK 40

The Mature Stage of Being Married

For the purpose of these discussions there are four stages of being married—the Establishment Phase (years 1–7), the Growth Stage (years 8–20), the Transition Stage (years 21–35), and the Mature Stage (years 36 and beyond). The Mature Stage of being married is a period in which some of the busyness of life begins to subside. Careers come to a close, children likely have their own lives, and changes in stamina slow things down physically. It is within this stage that circumstances allow, even require, more time for personal reflection.

This is a time when relevance and meaning is less defined by a packed daily schedule and more by the husband and wife rediscovering who they are as individuals. **This is a time when a couple can recommit to the enjoyment, support, and companionship to be found in one another.**

After thirty-six or more years of being married, a spiritual milestone has been reached by having maintained a steadfast relationship for such a long time. Your being together has gained the respect of others, especially those younger, through the fidelity and longevity evidenced by the many years of being married. If you find yourself in this stage of life, it is a time to be of benefit to other married couples through mentoring and sharing all that has been learned from having spent so many years together. This wisdom of hindsight can only be found and shared by couples who have been married a long time.

The Mature Stage of being married may continue for as long as you have already been married. It is not unheard of for couples to be married for seventy years! There is still plenty of time to grow and learn, but aspirations and expectations will tend to be more realistic and time-limited.

Seeking out and relying on what is really true in life will provide the strength, confidence, courage, optimism, and hope that a couple needs to sustain a mature relationship.

Managing Your Expectations

Everyone has expectations in life and love. We all have our own ideas about how things should be and how we want our life to turn out. Yet, it's when we don't know how to address our expectations—especially in being married—that we can easily end up feeling frustrated and disheartened.

Expectations are a very personal thing. When two people marry, each spouse brings their own set of expectations—things that are supposed to happen or be experienced. There are certain things a husband will expect from his wife, and there are certain things a wife will expect from her husband. More so, there are other things that each spouse might expect such as financial stability, parenthood, and shared interests.

The first step to managing marital expectations in a healthy and productive way is for a husband and wife to openly communicate about what they are looking for. **Understanding mutual expectations will help avoid the diversions and disappointments that can distract from the harmony that married couples seek.**

When you and your spouse are identifying and discussing your expectations with one another, it's important to remember that unless you make your expectations clear, you cannot expect your spouse to reach a full understanding of your needs and desires. For example, if one spouse is judging the relationship by standards that are unknown to the other spouse—frustration and conflict can arise.

When you are aware of your own expectations and those of your spouse, you create an opportunity for both of your expectations to be understood, respected, and, if necessary, modified.

Being Married and Religious Faith Go Together

God established being married as one way to fulfill his purposes on earth while at the same time creating a way to enrich life for those choosing to marry. In the New Testament, being married is even used as a metaphor to illustrate the relationship of Jesus to his body of believers, the church.

The essence of being married centers around a profound love of a husband and wife for one another, much like God's great love is the essence of his relationship with each of us—his creation. It is written in biblical Scripture that God is love, and to the extent a couple truly loves one another they experience a godly presence.

Maintaining religious faith and maintaining a good relationship involves the same elements of respect, redemption, communication, forgiveness, love, fidelity, and shared purpose. **When each spouse is committed to living out of biblically-based faith, being married will be able to realize its full potential for spiritual development.**

The efforts involved in honoring biblical truth and honoring a spouse are mutually reinforcing endeavors. Relational understanding and the experience of being married both improve when the teachings of the Bible are studied and followed.

Being married can be so much more than just companionship, estate, and children. Religious faith and being married can interact in such a way as to actually deepen both spiritual beliefs and the relationship of the two people.

What the Bible Teaches about Marital Compatibility (Part 1)

In reading the New Testament, you will find a letter that the apostle Paul wrote to the church in Ephesus. It contains a passage about being married that is challenging to understand.

In Ephesians 5:24, Paul writes that ". . . wives should submit to their husbands in everything." So what exactly does this mean? What is Paul trying to teach us about being married and the concept of submission?

Because the world and culture has changed dramatically since Paul wrote this passage, and because gender equality has become the accepted norm for most of western society, the idea that a wife is to categorically submit to the will of her husband is a notion that most women find difficult to accept and that most men dare not expect.

However, if what Paul wrote is considered in the larger context of Ephesians 5:21–33, you'll find that the authoritarian tone set forth in the one verse is actually softened when the letter is read in full. For example, the concept of submission as explained in Ephesians 5:21 becomes more of a *reciprocal obligation* of one believer to another.

If we look at what was happening within the historical time-frame and cultural climate of Paul's day, we come to understand that the Christian faith was to first and foremost be an example of peace. Paul was urging his fellow believers to avoid discord and to keep the domestic peace by encouraging wives to recognize the husband as the head of the household.

Paul made it clear, however, that this headship in the family by the husband was not a position to be used for domination or oppression. He wrote that a husband is to love his wife "as Christ loved the church and gave himself up for her. In this same way, husbands ought to love their wives as their own bodies."

In addition to Paul's message about submission, the apostle John quotes Jesus in his writing to establish that the relational standard for a married couple is to ". . . love each other as I have loved you" (John 15:12–13).

When there are questions about the concept of submission, it is most important to remember that there is but one to whom both a husband and the wife must submit, and that is Jesus Christ.

What the Bible Teaches about Marital Compatibility (Part 2)

In the Bible, you will find numerous teachings on being married and Christian living. In regard to these teachings, there are some passages that may result in confusion.

For example, the apostle Paul wrote in Galatians 3:28 that ". . . you are all one in Christ Jesus," yet in other instances Paul wrote that everyone must submit to the governing authorities and that wives in particular are to submit to their husbands in everything.

Given that we now live in a time where the concept of "submission" is often viewed contentiously between husbands and wives—how can you and your spouse reconcile such passages in the Bible?

Because husbands and wives are different both by virtue of their gender and personal autonomy, moral tension is to be expected whether you study the Bible's teachings or not. **Yet, despite the physical and emotional differences that exist between males and females, both are equal heirs and citizens of the kingdom of God in heaven and upon the earth.**

If you and your spouse have experienced conflict over differing views on biblical Scriptures that reference being married, one action that can help ease this tension is for both you and your spouse to commit to pursuing positions that foster peace.

In Matthew 5:9, Jesus says, "Blessed are the peacemakers, for they will be called sons of God." Paul reinforces this wisdom teaching of Jesus' when he is writing to the Romans. He writes, "If it is possible, as far as it depends on you, live at peace with everyone" (Romans 12:18). And, even the writer of Hebrews wrote, "Make every effort to live in peace with all men, and to be holy . . ." (Hebrews 12:14).

There is no need for chaos where a Christian brother and sister of equal standing in Christ are attempting to establish a meaningful relationship within the context of their culture, their expectations of one another, and their attempt to be faithful to biblical teachings.

At the end of the day, the ultimate goal in being married should be peace and not dominance. Mutual submission in the pursuit of peace is an exhibition of humility, love, respect, and obedience, thus mutual submission between a husband and wife should be embraced and not feared.

What the Bible Teaches about Marital Compatibility (Part 3)

In the context of Colossians 3:18–19, submission in being married is a reciprocal act and required of both husbands and wives. In this particular Scripture, the apostle Paul's instruction to a wife centers on the obligation she has to submit to her husband; however, he makes it clear that her primary obligation is to first and foremost follow and practice the teachings of Jesus.

A wife's submission to her husband should always be contingent upon due respect. Her act of submission should never place her in psychological, physical, or spiritual harm, or put her in legal jeopardy.

But Paul also instructs the husband to practice submission. When a husband practices submission, his requirement is to love his wife as defined in 1 Corinthians 13, and to never abuse his headship by being harsh with his spouse.

Contrary to many distorted interpretations on the concept of submission, the most important thing to understand is that submission is a mutual and reciprocal act required by both spouses. When this is understood, a husband's ascribed headship in the family becomes less about the exercise of authority and more about nurturing and leadership.

While being married, there is no room for authoritarian suppression or control. And if you want your relationship to model true biblical teachings, then both you and your spouse need to understand that real submission is reflected in a life lived in service to one another.

Being Married is Not the Measure of Personal Worth

Being married can be one of the most validating, enriching experiences that life has to offer. Sharing the companionship of a spouse who loves you, desires your company, and seeks the best for you can help sustain a deep sense of personal well-being. On the other hand, nothing can be more demoralizing or create feelings of personal failure, rejection, or worthlessness than a failure at being married.

Your personal identity and the awareness of your self-worth should be brought into being married, not created by being married. And when the Bible teaches about the oneness of being married, it centers on the unity of purpose, not a consolidation of two individual personalities into one.

As individual identity and worth may be strengthened through being married, a person's worth and value should not be destroyed by divorce. In order to remain emotionally, mentally, and spiritually intact regardless of life's circumstances, a person's significance and life's meaning must be anchored in a sound self-concept, not the adoration of a spouse or pride in being married.

Healthy concepts of personal spirituality have been communicated to us by our divine creator in the form of Scripture written by inspired writers and recorded in both the Old and New Testaments of the Bible. And within the Bible, there is no question that the ultimate message of Scripture affirms that all people have irrevocable and immeasurable value and worth, no matter what life brings.

Personal failure is forgivable and a disrupted life is recoverable, but only if one's self-condemnation does not obscure the redemption promised through belief in the life and teachings of Jesus Christ.

Being Married Is More Than Just Talent

Talent is a skill or trait that comes naturally. The expression of a talent is usually very spontaneous, even unconscious. Talent can be fulfilling and beneficial to the talented one, and such talent can be impressive, useful, and enjoyable to others. Pure talent can be admired in many settings, but not always in being married.

Being married requires that two people be very aware of their personal and collective circumstances and be very tuned in as to how to best meet the needs of one another. Thoughts and actions that come to a person naturally, things for which there is great skill, can be lived out where there is little effort and forethought and thus be ill-timed or inappropriate in a given circumstance.

Talent, especially involving personality traits, can become the unintended default for how one might deal with the demands of being married or the specific needs of a spouse. Talent can become a habitual response to every situation. If the husband or wife is just naturally entertaining, productive, attentive, enduring, persuasive, or consoling, particular circumstances may call for actions that go beyond this default. Circumstances may require one or both of the spouses to exercise an attentiveness or responsiveness that is beyond the area of their natural talent.

If you are entertaining, don't use this gift for distraction when there is emotional work to be done. If you are productive, learn to read when the family needs a rest. If you are attentive, don't be afraid of tough love when it is needed. If you are enduring, come clean with your spouse when something is bothering you. If you are persuasive, don't use this talent to talk your way out of a fault. If you are consoling, don't create emotional cover for the dysfunctional behavior of loved ones.

Talent will only be beneficial in a relationship when it is used thoughtfully.

The Discipline of Discernment

Discernment is the process of going about making an appropriate decision. In a perfect world, discernment is about gathering as much pertinent information as possible and considering this information thoroughly and objectively over a period of time before making a decision or forming an opinion. Discernment is methodically and with an open mind choosing from among competing options.

From time to time, both a husband and wife will have to address whether the issue at hand is centered on sizzle or substance. That is, there will always be the challenge of discerning what things are merely attractive and what things are really necessary. Whether it's real estate, exotic vacations, nice cars, or stylish clothes, each spouse should attempt to discern whether the things desired are rooted in truth or fiction. For instance, it will take discernment to choose between buying a new car and funding an IRA or paying down what is owed on the credit card.

Discernment is being thoughtful, and there is no circumstance on earth where thoughtfulness is as needed and appreciated as in being married. Discernment is not about power, opinions, or strength of will. It is when you are letting the process of inquiry lead you toward decisions that will honor what is true and right. Taking this approach will honor both you and your spouse.

If you and your spouse want to become more discerning in your decision making, it will require effort, patience, and an inquiring mind. **It will require both of you to be confident in letting objective information take the lead rather than searching for information that will reinforce a preferred point of view.**

There is always an element of wisdom in any attempt to make a discerning decision, and there is no better place to learn about living a good life than the Bible.

WEEK 49

Emotional Divorce

Indifference is toxic to any marriage. Contrasted to hostility or abuse, indifference is to be uncaring, inattentive, or withholding of one's self. Indifference can result in a couple living separate lives while still sharing the same name and living in the same house.

When the interaction between a husband and wife becomes more transactional than emotional, it will hurt the marriage and leave each partner feeling isolated, unfulfilled, and lonely. And if it's duty that is holding a marriage together—more than desire—it is likely that an emotional divorce has already taken place.

An emotional divorce has taken place when there is more endurance than enthusiasm, more coping than kindness, more disgust than dignity, and more pragmatism than promise. And, when civility is as close as a couple can get to respect, there is little room for experiencing joy.

An emotional divorce involves no lawyers, no court, and no decrees. Rather, it is a created state that results in as much pain and disruption for everyone as if the marriage were legally dissolved. The combination of denial, dysfunction, and disdain creates a toxic mix that will poison a marriage.

Sometimes emotional distance cannot be reduced even by the hard work of a couple trying to repair the damage to their marriage. Help from a qualified third-party may be necessary to reverse this destructive trend and create a pathway toward reconnection. If the emotional distance between a husband and wife has not been too far for too long, there is always hope that hard work, using good information, and competent guidance will result in revitalizing a marriage. A good outcome will certainly be worth the effort!

WEEK 50

Happiness and Being Married

What should being married feel like? Is being married a good thing if a couple is not happy? Is feeling happy the best measure of being married? Being happy in life and in being married is a good thing, but being happy is not always possible.

Being married is intended to be a partnership where two people pool their resources and experiences in facing the challenges of life, but this special relationship does not exempt anyone from sadness and hardship, nor does it make adversity any easier to bear. Many a couple have survived, even thrived, during times of war, economic depression, unemployment, illness, moral failure, and lengthy separation. How is this possible?

It may well be that the best feeling for a married couple is that of being anchored and at peace. **A feeling of confidence in one another and in the source of their hope and direction may actually be preferable to a feeling of happiness.** With the right frame of reference and a realistic expectation about life, a couple can experience a sense of well-being—even when there is hardship—when they are able to work constructively together through better or worse, richer or poorer, in sickness and in health.

Could it be that to look for happiness in being married is to settle for something less than is otherwise possible in the relationship? Is there a state of being married that transcends mere happiness and that can actually be more endearing to the relationship over the long-run?

Action Must Follow Belief

Beliefs based upon the biblical teachings about life and about the relationship between a husband and wife are good nutrients with which to feed being married. Good information provides strong building blocks for the foundation of any lifelong relationship. However, beliefs alone, even if scripturally-based, are not the guarantee of a good marital experience, nor will they be able to prevent trouble and divorce. The rate of divorce among Christian believers is about the same as the divorce rate among the general population. What is missing?

Knowledge about being married creates the standard, but it takes something more than just knowing and agreeing how being married should work in order to actually have a good relationship. Beliefs based upon knowledge must be allowed to challenge ways of thinking, change behaviors, alter lifestyles, promote good will, permit forgiveness, encourage humility, and support sacrifice. Beliefs only held at an intellectual level, even where the facts are correct and even if based upon biblical Scripture, will not by themselves generate the personal transformation that is necessary for a couple to relate to one another in ways that will result in a mutually meaningful experience.

Knowledge-based beliefs must result in changes in ways of thinking and acting that actually support the belief. Beliefs that are to make any difference must be accompanied by courage, conviction, dedication, and action. Where well-founded beliefs become part of a relational foundation, the basis for constructive and supportive action will be present to provide what a couple needs to stand up to the challenges inherent in being married.

WEEK 52

In Defense of Being Married

Being married does not look the same across different cultures and differing faith groups. The defense of this unique relationship is much more than a political, religious, or intellectual proposition. The ultimate defense of being married is in how well it works.

Western culture does not honor being married in the same way as the Bible. The cultural definition and expectation of being married leans toward and promotes what is expedient and pragmatic, not what is constructive, exemplary, or lasting. For these reasons, **the best defense of being married as a biblical concept does not reside in a skillfully worded definition, the strict administration of religious orthodoxy, or sweeping legislation but in a good example.**

The best defense of being married in the biblical sense does not take place in a meeting or in a voting booth. The best defense of being married takes place in the bedroom, around the kitchen table, on a vacation with the family, and during the time with friends. The claims made in defense of the biblical model for being married are best validated for others, especially children, when they see this life partnership actually working—validated when they see that being married is a nurturing, functional, and safe model for a lifetime relationship.

A good example will always be the best defense of the biblical pattern for being married.

References and Endorsements

REFERENCES RELATED TO SECTION 3: COMMUNICATION AND TOPICS FOR DISCUSSION

All Scriptures are taken from the 2011 Edition of the New International Version (NIV) of the New Testament and Hebrew Bible. Paraphrases taken from *The Message* will be designated as MSG at the end of the quotation.

Week 1: Constructive Confrontation
Ephesians 4:22–24

"You were taught, with regard to your former way of life, to put off your old self, which is being corrupted by its deceitful desires; to be made new in the attitude of your minds; and to put on the new self, created to be like God in true righteousness and holiness."

Week 2: Whose Truth?
Proverbs 15:22; Psalms 32:8; 2 Timothy 3:16–17

"Plans fail for lack of counsel, but with many advisers they succeed."

"I will instruct you and teach you in the way you should go; I will counsel you with my loving eye on you."

"All Scripture is God-breathed and is useful for teaching, rebuking, correcting and training in righteousness, so that the man of God may be thoroughly equipped for every good work."

Week 3: Partnership in Being Married
Matthew 19:6

"So they are no longer two, but one flesh. Therefore what God has joined together, let no one separate."

Week 4: Planning for the Journey of Being Married
Colossians 2:5

"For though I am absent from you in body, I am present with you in spirit and delight to see how orderly you are and how firm your faith in Christ is."

Week 5: Giving and Receiving While Being Married
Acts 20:35; Colossians 3:18–19; Hebrews 4:16

"In everything I did, I showed you that by this kind of hard work we must help the weak, remembering the words the Lord Jesus himself said: 'It is more blessed to give than to receive.'"

"Wives, understand and support your husbands by submitting to them in ways that honor the Master. Husbands, go all out in love for your wives. Don't take advantage of them." (MSG)

"Let us then approach the throne of grace with confidence, so that we may receive mercy and find grace to help us in our time of need."

Week 6: Being Married Is a Sacred Design
Genesis 2:18; Genesis 2:24

"The Lord God said, 'It is not good for the man to be alone. I will make a helper suitable for him.'"

"That is why a man leaves his father and mother and is united to his wife, and they become one flesh."

Week 7: Why Is Being Married Easier for Some Couples?
Matthew 7:12; 1 Peter 5:5b

"So in everything, do to others what you would have them do to you, for this sums up the Law and the Prophets."

"All of you, clothe yourselves with humility toward one another, because, 'God opposes the proud but shows favor to the humble.'"

Week 8: What's the Main Thing in Being Married?
1 Corinthians 3:10b–13a

"But each one should build with care. For no one can lay any foundation other than the one already laid, which is Jesus Christ. If anyone builds on this foundation using gold, silver, costly stones, wood, hay or straw, their work will be shown for what it is, because the Day will bring it to light."

Week 9: The Foundation for Being Married
1 Corinthians 1:27–31

"But God chose the foolish things of the world to shame the wise; God chose the weak things of the world to shame the strong. God chose the lowly things of this world and the despised things—and the things that are not—to nullify the things that are, so that no one may boast before him. It is because of him that you are in Christ Jesus, who has become for us wisdom from God—that is, our righteousness, holiness and redemption. Therefore, as it is written: 'Let him who boasts boast in the Lord.'"

Week 10: The Establishment Stage of Being Married
1 Corinthians 3:10–13

"By the grace God has given me, I laid a foundation as a wise builder, and someone else is building on it. But each one should build with care. For no one can lay any foundation other than the one already laid, which is Jesus Christ. If anyone builds on this foundation using gold, silver, costly stones, wood, hay

or straw, his work will be shown for what it is, because the Day will bring it to light. It will be revealed with fire, and the fire will test the quality of each person's work."

Week 11: Trust Is a Must
2 Corinthians 4:1–2

"Therefore, since through God's mercy we have this ministry, we do not lose heart. Rather, we have renounced secret and shameful ways; we do not use deception, nor do we distort the word of God. On the contrary, by setting forth the truth plainly we commend ourselves to everyone's conscience in the sight of God."

Week 12: A Laboratory for Grace
Hebrews 12:14–15

"Make every effort to live in peace with everyone and to be holy; without holiness no one will see the Lord. See to it that no one falls short of the grace of God and that no bitter root grows up to cause trouble and defile many."

Week 13: A Source for Wisdom in Being Married
Ephesians 3:20

"Now to him who is able to do immeasurably more than all we ask or imagine, according to his power that is at work within us."

Week 14: Practicing Being Present
Matthew 13:14b–15

"You will be ever hearing but never understanding; you will be ever seeing but never perceiving. For this people's heart has become calloused; they hardly hear with their ears, and they have closed their eyes. Otherwise they might see with their eyes, hear with their ears, understand with their hearts and turn, and I would heal them."

Week 15: It's All about You!
Acts 3:19; 1 John 1:9

"Repent, then, and turn to God, so that your sins may be wiped out, that times of refreshing may come from the Lord."

"If we confess our sins, he is faithful and just and will forgive us our sins and purify us from all unrighteousness."

Week 16: Listening for Learning
James 1:19

"My dear brothers and sisters, take note of this: Everyone should be quick to listen, slow to speak and slow to become angry."

Week 17: Happiness: It's Up to You
Galatians 6:4–5

"Each one should test their own actions. Then they can take pride in themselves alone, without comparing themselves to someone else, for each one should carry their own load."

Week 18: Biblical Teaching on Being Married (Part 1)
Galatians 3:28; Ephesians 5:22–24; Ephesians 5:25

"There is neither Jew nor Greek, slave nor free, nor is there male and female, for you are all one in Christ Jesus."

"Wives, submit to your husbands as you do to the Lord. For the husband is the head of the wife as Christ is the head of the church, his body, of which he is the Savior. Now as the church submits to Christ, so also wives should submit to their husbands in everything."

"Husbands, love your wives, just as Christ loved the church and gave himself up for her."

Week 19: Biblical Teaching on Being Married (Part 2)
2 Timothy 3:16

"All Scripture is God-breathed and is useful for teaching, rebuking, correcting and training in righteousness."

Week 20: The Growth Stage of Being Married
Ephesians 4:14–16

"Then we will no longer be infants, tossed back and forth by the waves, and blown here and there by every wind of teaching and by the cunning and craftiness of people in their deceitful scheming. Instead, speaking the truth in love, we will grow to becomes in every respect the mature body of him who is the Head, that is, Christ. From him the whole body, joined and held together by every supporting ligament, grows and builds itself up in love, as each part does its work."

Week 21: Children and Being Married (Part 1)
Proverbs 11:29a

"Whoever brings ruin on their family will inherit only wind."

Week 22: Children and Being Married (Part 2)
Proverbs 22:6

"Start children off on the way they should go, and even when they are old they will not turn from it."

Week 23: Children and Being Married (Part 3)
Ephesians 6:4

"Fathers, do not exasperate your children; instead, bring them up in the training and instruction of the Lord."

Week 24: Laughter: The Best Medicine
Philippians 4:4

"Rejoice in the Lord always. I will say it again: Rejoice!"

Week 25: Being Married as Teamwork
Ephesians 5:31

"For this reason a man will leave his father and mother and be united to his wife, and the two will become one flesh."

Week 26: Vulnerability in Being Married
Matthew 5:16

"Keep open house; be generous with your lives. By opening up to others, you'll prompt people to open up with God, this generous Father in heaven." (MSG)

Week 27: Wisdom from 350 Years of Being Married (Part 1)
Proverbs 15:22

"Plans fail for lack of counsel, but with many advisers they succeed."

Week 28: Wisdom from 350 Years of Being Married (Part 2)
Proverbs 15:22

"Plans fail for lack of counsel, but with many advisers they succeed."

Week 30: The Transition Stage of Being Married
James 3:17

"But the wisdom that comes from heaven is first of all pure; then peace-loving, considerate, submissive, full of mercy and good fruit, impartial and sincere."

Week 31: Managing Your Emotions
2 Corinthians 13:5

"Test yourselves to make sure you are solid in the faith. Don't drift along taking everything for granted. Give yourselves regular checkups. You need firsthand evidence, not mere hearsay, that Jesus Christ is in you. Test it out. If you fail the test, do something about it." (MSG)

Week 32: Making Things Worse
Matthew 18:21–22

"Then Peter came to Jesus and asked, 'Lord, how many times shall I forgive my brother or sister when who sins against me? Up to seven times?' Jesus answered, 'I tell you, not seven times, but seventy-seven times.'"

Week 33: Unfaithfulness in Being Married
Malachi 2:15–17

"Has not the one God made them you? You belong to him in body and spirit. And what does the one God seek? Godly offspring. So be on your guard, and do not be unfaithful to the wife of your youth. 'The man who hates and divorces his wife,' says the Lord, the God of Israel, 'does violence to the one he should protect,' says the Lord Almighty. So by on your guard and do not be unfaithful."

Week 34: The Goal Is Reconciliation
Matthew 5:9; 1 Peter 3:8

"Blessed are the peacemakers, for they will be called children of God."

"Finally, all of you, be like-minded, be sympathetic, love one another, be compassionate and humble."

Week 35: What Sex While Being Married Is Not (Part 1)
Matthew 6:25–26

"Therefore I tell you, do not worry about your life, what you will eat or drink; or about your body, what you will wear. Is not life more than food, and the body more than clothes? Look at the birds of the air; they do not sow or reap or store away in barns, and yet your heavenly Father feeds them. Are you not much more valuable than they?"

Week 36: What Sex While Being Married Is Not (Part 2)
1 Corinthians 13:4–8a

"Love is patient, love is kind. It does not envy, it does not boast, it is not proud. It does not dishonor others, it is not self-seeking, it is not easily angered, it keeps no record of wrongs. Love does not delight in evil but rejoices with the truth. It always protects, always trusts, always hopes, always perseveres. Love never fails."

Week 37: What Sex While Being Married Is Not (Part 3)
1 Corinthians 7:3–5a

"The husband should fulfill his marital duty to his wife, and likewise the wife to her husband. The wife does not have authority over her own body but yields it to her husband. In the same way, the husband does not have authority over his own body but yields it to his wife. Do not deprive each other except perhaps by mutual consent."

Week 38: Finding the Value in Being Married
Romans 12:9–10

"Love must be sincere. Hate what is evil; cling to what is good. Be devoted to one another in love. Honor one another above yourselves."

Week 39: Peace While Being Married
Acts 2:37–39; James 3:17

"When the people heard this, they were cut to the heart and said to Peter and the other apostles, 'Brothers, what shall we do?' Peter replied, 'Repent and be baptized, every one of you, in the name of Jesus Christ for the forgiveness of your sins. And you will receive the gift of the Holy Spirit. The promise is for you and your children and for all who are far off—for all whom the Lord our God will call.'"

"But the wisdom that comes from heaven is first of all pure; then peace-loving, considerate, submissive, full of mercy and good fruit, impartial and sincere."

Week 40: The Mature Stage of Being Married
Psalms 71:20–21; 1 Peter 5:10–11

"Though you have made me see troubles, many and bitter, you will restore my life again; from the depths of the earth you will again bring me up. You will increase my honor and comfort me once more."

"And the God of all grace, who called you to his eternal glory in Christ, after you have suffered a little while, will himself restore you and make you strong, firm and steadfast. To him be the power forever and ever. Amen."

Week 41: Managing Your Expectations
1 Corinthians 1:27–31

"But God chose the foolish things of the world to shame the wise; God chose the weak things of the world to shame the strong. He chose the lowly things of this world and the despised things—and the things that are not—to nullify the things that are, so that no one may boast before him. It is because of him that you are in Christ Jesus, who has become for us wisdom from God—that is, our righteousness, holiness and redemption. Therefore, as it is written: 'Let him who boasts boast in the Lord.'"

Week 42: Being Married and Religious Faith Go Together
Ephesians 5:31–33

"For this reason a man will leave his father and mother and be united to his wife, and the two will become one flesh. This is a profound mystery—but I am talking about Christ and the church. However, each one of you also must love his wife as he loves himself, and the wife must respect her husband."

Week 43: What the Bible Teaches about Marital Compatibility (Part 1)
John 15:12–13; Ephesians 5:21

"My command is this: Love each other as I have loved you. Greater love has no one than this: to lay down one's life for one's friends."

"Submit to one another out of reverence for Christ."

Week 44: What the Bible Teaches about Marital Compatibility (Part 2)
Galatians 3:28

"There is neither Jew nor Greek, neither slave nor free, nor is there male and female, for you are all one in Christ Jesus."

Week 45: What the Bible Teaches about Marital Compatibility (Part 3)
Colossians 3:15–19

"Let the peace of Christ rule in your hearts, since as members of one body you were called to peace. And be thankful. Let the word of Christ dwell in you richly as you teach and admonish one another with all wisdom through psalms, hymns, and songs from the Spirit, singing to God with gratitude in your hearts. And whatever you do, whether in word or deed, do it all in the name of the Lord Jesus, giving thanks to God the Father through him."

Week 46: Being Married Is Not the Measure of Personal Worth
2 Peter 1:3–4

"His divine power has given us everything we need for a godly life through our knowledge of him who called us by his own glory and goodness. Through these he has given us his very great and precious promises, so that through them you may participate in the divine nature and escape the corruption in the world caused by evil desires."

Week 47: Being Married Is More Than Just Talent
Luke 12:48b

"From everyone who has been given much, much will be demanded, and from the one who has been entrusted with much, much more will be asked."

Week 48: The Discipline of Discernment
Hebrews 4:12

"For the word of God is living and active. Sharper than any double-edged sword, it penetrates even to dividing soul and spirit, joints and marrow; it judges the thoughts and attitudes of the heart."

Week 49: Emotional Divorce
Ephesians 4:29–32

"Do not let any unwholesome talk come out of your mouths, but only what is helpful for building others up according to their needs, that it may benefit those who listen. And do not grieve the Holy Spirit of God, with whom you were sealed for the day of redemption. Get rid of all bitterness, rage and anger, brawling and slander, along with every form of malice. Be kind and compassionate to one another, forgiving each other, just as in Christ God forgave you."

Week 50: Happiness and Being Married
James 1:2–4

"Consider it pure joy, my brothers and sisters, whenever you face trials of many kinds, because you know that the testing of your faith develops perseverance. Let perseverance finish its work so that you may be mature and complete, not lacking anything."

Week 51: Action Must Follow Belief
James 2:17

"Isn't it obvious that God-talk without God-acts is outrageous nonsense?" (MSG)

Week 52: In Defense of Being Married
1 Peter 2:12

"Live such good lives among the pagans that, though they accuse you of doing wrong, they may see your good deeds and glorify God on the day he visits us."

ENDORSEMENTS RELATED TO SECTION 2: THE CORE STORY PROCESS

Dr. Terry Smith's Core Story technique provides a kind and caring way to give people a revealing and valuable look at themselves. The Core Story also creates a unique opportunity for a person to discover and acknowledge their Core Beliefs and the powerful role these beliefs have in shaping a person's life.

> — Joseph McLoughlin, Ph.D., Associate Professor of the Practice of Psychology and Human Development at Vanderbilt University

As someone who went through the process of recounting my Core Story with Dr. Terry Smith almost two decades ago, I know personally that it can be a powerful experience. In this booklet, he goes step by step through his approach to drawing out the Core Story which highlights special relationships and controlling beliefs. It instructs the reader on how to replicate the process he has developed to transform lives over his many years as a counselor.

— Trina R. Shanks, Ph.D., Associate Professor,
University of Michigan, School of Social Work

The Core Story provides insight into broken attachments and the meaning we place on those family attachments we experienced as children. Through the tool, we learn what we had to do to get our needs met! I think this should be an excellent accompaniment to addiction treatment.

— Leslie S.C. Cole, M.D., Author of *Quit Pain Pills Without the*
Withdrawal: How to Break Free from Your Dependence and
Finally Wake Up Feeling Normal

The Core Story process gives a person the sacred space to tell the truth about themselves. When I experienced the process, it was both profound and humbling. For those seeking greater understanding about human relationships, the Core Story coaching tool is a tremendous gift that offers endless possibilities to experience understanding, healing, and draw us to a deeper readiness to give and receive love.

— Karen Casey, M.Ed., Educator, Metro Nashville Public Schools

The Core Story process is a practical tool that will be used by persons from a variety of backgrounds to help others. Mental health specialists will see the Core Story's value almost immediately. Physicians and therapists will use it with profit. It guides leaders and trusted persons in opening safe dialogue in which another can discover and begin to (re)structure their life.

— Rubel Shelly, Ph.D., author of
Divorce and Remarriage: A Redemptive Theology

Every man, woman, and child has a Core Story. Unlocking that story, understanding the unconscious drivers, and discovering the true self has freed thousands from addictive and obsessive behaviors. On the job and in countless marriages, those behaviors sabotage success. The Core Story manual speeds the process of discovery and is an important tool for recovery.

— Russell Bloodworth, Jr., Executive Vice-President of
Boyle Investment, Inc.

The Core Story is an enhanced approach to using the genogram. This insightful and spiritually grounded process allows individuals to see themselves through a hopeful and true lens. Working with the Core Story is a great beginning and provides a solid foundation for continued emotional and spiritual healing and growth.

— Lezlie R. Owsley, MMFT, LMFT,
Intentional Life Counseling, LLC

If you have experienced the genogram as a resource for understanding one's family system, what Dr. Terry Smith has developed with the Core Story tool is more life giving and transformative than the genogram by itself! I've been personally transformed by the Core Story and have also witnessed the sacred space created with others each time a colleague, client, or friend experiences their Core Story. The Core Story helps people better understand the heart of human relationships.

— John O. York, Ph.D., Director, Doctor of Ministry Program,
Associate Dean, Hozelip School of Theology,
Lipscomb University

Core Story is a powerful instrument for discovery and healing of deep trauma. It is particularly valuable for those suffering PTSD from military or first responder experiences.

— Larry Malone, Retired Captain, USN Aviator,
Vietnam War Veteran

Several years ago, I had the pleasure of Terry Smith facilitating my Core Story amongst two friends. I was blown away by the things that I learned about myself. The Core Story tool shined a light on my Core Beliefs, Core Wounds, and Core Lies. I have since been able to confront my inadequacies and draw closer to the One who loves me and also help others process their life journey by facilitating their Core Story. The tool is powerful and illuminating as it allows individuals to look in the rearview mirror of their life and understand "great and unsearchable things they did not know."

— William Roberts, Story Archeologists, Retired Business Executive

Reading Resources

SECTION 1: THE INFLUENCE OF CORE BELIEFS ON BEING MARRIED

Chapman, Gary, *The Five Love Languages*

Feldhahn, Shaunti, *Highly Happy Marriages*

Foster, Richard, *Celebration of Discipline*

Gottman, John, *The Seven Principles for Making Marriage Work*

Keller, Timothy, *The Meaning of Marriage*

Miller, Sherod; Miller, Phyllis A.; Nunnally, Elam W.; Wackman, Daniel B., *Talking and Listening Together, Couple Communication 1*

Mulholland, Jr., M. Robert, *Shaped by the Word*

Neuman, M. Gary, *Emotional Infidelity*

Pillemer, Karl, Ph.D., *30 Lessons for Loving*

Runkel, Hal E., *The Self-Centered Marriage*

Shelly, Rubel, *Divorce and Remarriage*

Stanley, Scott M. and Trathen, Daniel, *A Lasting Promise*

Thomas, Gary, *Sacred Marriage*

Tournier, Paul, *To Understand Each Other*

Vernick, Leslie, *The Emotionally Destructive Marriage*

SECTION 2: THE CORE STORY PROCESS

Bloodworth Jr., Russell, *Visions, Dreams & Encounters*

Bowen, Murray and Michael Kerr, *Family Evaluation*

Friedman, Edwin, *Generation to Generation*

Jordan, Merle, *Reclaiming Your Story*

Jordan, Merle, *Taking on the Gods*

Keating, Thomas, *Invitation to Love*

Keating, Thomas, *Open Mind, Open Heart*

Litz, Brett T.; Lebowitz, Leslie; Gray, Matt J.; Nash, William P., *Adaptive Disclosure: A New Treatment for Military Trauma, Loss, and Moral Injury*

Meninger, William A., *The Process of Forgiveness*

Payne, Leeanne, *Heaven's Calling: A Memoir of One's Steep Ascent*

Rohr, Richard, *Divine Dance*

Rohr, Richard, *Falling Upward*

Saunders, Landon, *Life Loves to Happen No Matter What Happens*

Saunders, Landon, website On Being Human at https://www.obhuman.com

Seamands, David, *Healing Damaged Emotions*

Smith, Terry S., *Delta Blues: From Darkness to Light*

Smith, Terry S., website Coaching: Life Matters at www.coachinglifematters.com

Snodgrass, Klyne, *Who God Says You Are*

Van Der Kolk, Bessel, M.D., *The Body Keeps the Score*

Willard, Dallas, *Divine Conspiracy*

Woodroof, James, *Sayings That Saved My Sanity*

Made in the USA
Coppell, TX
02 September 2022

82473004R00122